New 5 Step Budgeting Program!
Gain the Motivation, Knowledge and Discipline To...

Get a GRASP on Your Budget and Your Cash!

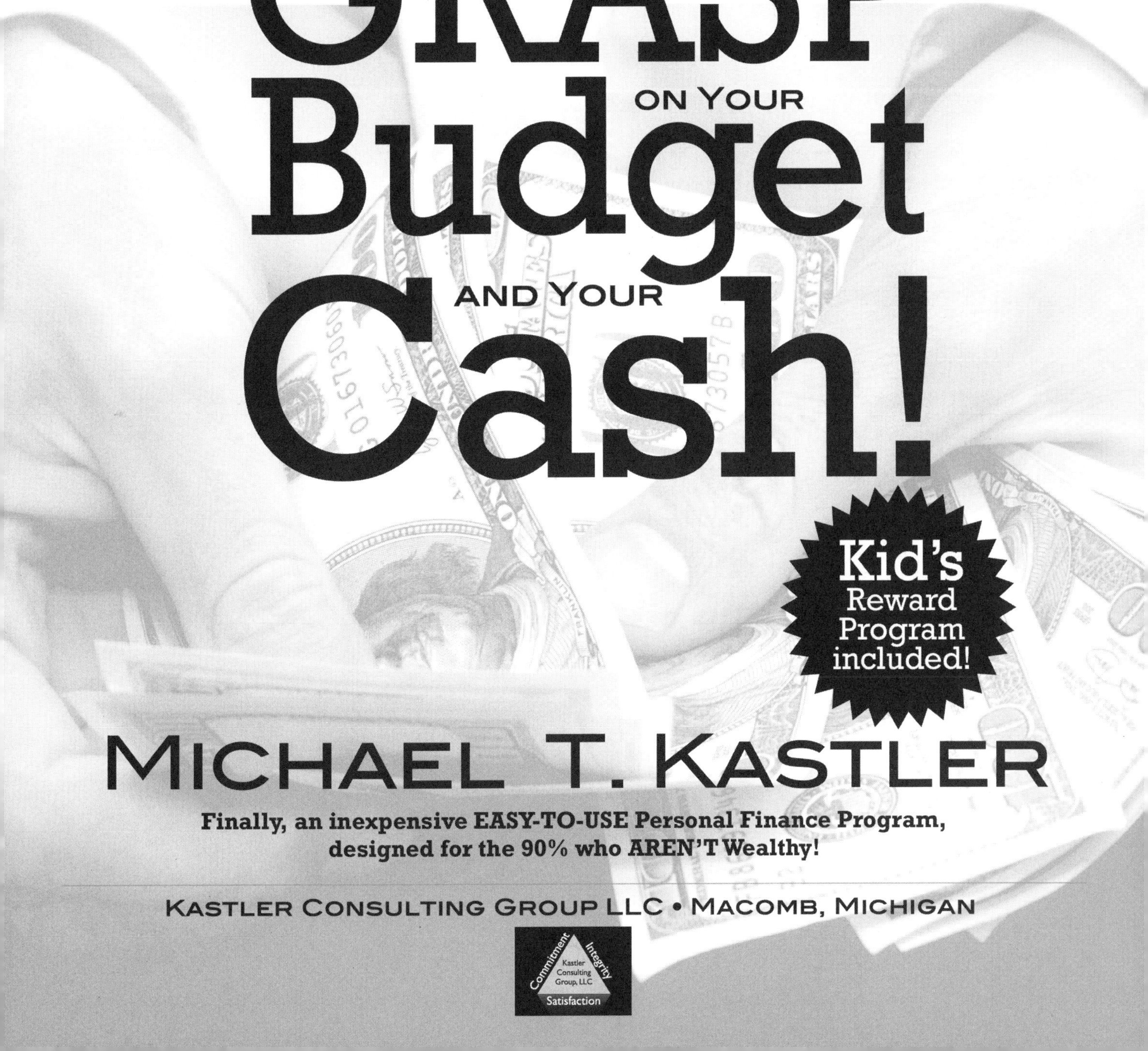

Kid's Reward Program included!

MICHAEL T. KASTLER

Finally, an inexpensive EASY-TO-USE Personal Finance Program, designed for the 90% who AREN'T Wealthy!

Kastler Consulting Group LLC • Macomb, Michigan

Commitment Integrity Kastler Consulting Group, LLC Satisfaction

"Get a GRASP"
on your Budget and your Cash!
Finally, an Inexpensive and Easy-to-Use Personal Finance Program
Designed for the 90% that aren't Wealthy!

- 2nd Edition -

by Michael T. Kastler

This publication is designed to provide the reader with the knowledge, process, and tools in regard to personal budgeting. It is sold with the understanding that the author and publisher are not engaged in the rendering of professional financial planning services, legal, accounting, or other professional services. If these types of services are required, a competent professional should be sought.

All Scripture quotations taken from the *King James Version* of ***The Holy Bible*** unless otherwise noted.

ISBN (13): 978-0-578-03797-4

Library of Congress Control Number: 2009911353

Kastler Consulting Group, LLC
51194 Romeo Plank Rd., Suite #412
Macomb, MI 48042

Edited/Proofread by: Eugenia Orr, I4 Expressions
Original Cover Design by: Benjamin Carr, Uno Global Solutions
Cover & Interior Design by: LaTanya Orr, Selah Branding and Design

Printed in the United States of America

DEDICATION

This publication is dedicated to my two children, who have learned the importance of developing a responsible personal spending plan and budget. Also, to all the people who came through other financial planning programs with me, still struggling with developing their monthly budget. I designed this for all of them and anyone else looking for a practical, easy and quick way to do your budgeting by removing the apprehension and putting a little fun back in.

TABLE OF CONTENTS

PREFACE

Welcome to the **"Get a GRASP..."** method of personal financial budgeting. The purpose of this workbook is to assist individuals in getting a grasp of their personal financial situation. It is not intended as a program to make recommendations to get rich quick or any other false promises. By getting a **"GRASP"** of your assets, income, debts, and monthly expenses, you will be able to see where your money is and where it's going. This is a great tool you can use on a monthly basis to manage your budget and institute a plan to pay off debt quickly and build wealth over time by saving regularly.

This program was inspired by many years of my personal financial journey, during which I've used most of the commercially-available financial tools. Most were "all-encompassing" tools that did much more than what I needed and fell short of what I was looking for: an easy-to-use, fast and inexpensive tool to manage my budget. After hours of frustration with those programs, I would always end up using my own budget forms and Microsoft Excel (MS Excel) spreadsheet.

A second inspiration came recently after leading five small groups of people from my church, through a nationally-renowned, 12-week personal finance program. Overall, the program was very well done, covering a broad range of financial topics including budgeting, debt, emergency fund, mutual funds, insurance, real estate, etc. I believe everyone walked away a lot smarter. However, I found that after attending the 12-week program, many people were still struggling with developing their budgets. The forms, process, and the electronic version (which was very expensive) were just too complicated.

Hence, I developed the 1st Edition 5-step process, **"Get a GRASP..."** for creating a spending plan or budget. It is robust enough for nearly everyone to benefit from with easy-to-use and inexpensive tools for managing a budget. My goal was to package a workbook, hard copy forms, and MS Excel spreadsheet at a very reasonable cost so that anyone could afford it, without straining their budget! The 5-step **"Get a GRASP..."** process is the "knowledge," and primary basis for the 1st edition.

In this newly expanded 2nd edition, I've added a "motivation" section and a "discipline" section. In the motivation section, I convey why personal budgeting is important, how to get motivated, set goals, how to differentiate needs vs wants, and how to make decisions. To round out the whole process, the "discipline" section provides the tools for consistency and tracking progress over time.

When I put the three sections together, you can see how interdependent they are. The knowledge can't be applied without the motivation. And the whole process isn't complete without the discipline to keep going from month to month.

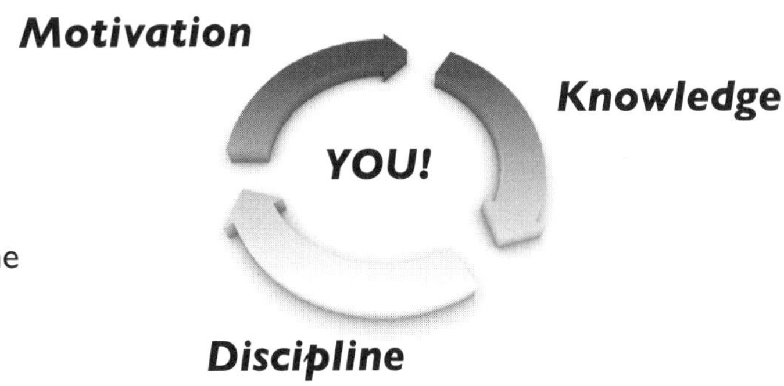

I am very excited to offer this robust, yet easy-to-use program to everyone that isn't already wealthy, which is about 90% of the American population.

I hope you enjoy this program and put it to good practical use. I am always interested in feedback to improve this program. You can email me your thoughts at mkastler@kastlerconsultinggroup.com.

Happy Budgeting!

PART I
MOTIVATION

BUILDING YOUR FOUNDATION

"And in the end, it's not the years in your life that count.
It's the life in your years."
- Abraham Lincoln -

In these first three chapters, I will identify some key motivators for you to put a spending plan or personal budgeting on the top of your priority list, take the fear out of the budgeting process, and explain how to get started.

I start with the **Motivators** section because if you are not motivated, nothing will happen! You can maximize the "life in your years" by gaining control of personal finances, eliminating debt, and watching financial goals come to fruition.

Just as all good homebuilders start their home designs and building process with a blueprint that meets the homeowner's motivations and goals, you too can build your financial plan on solid foundation with your motivations and goals as a blueprint for getting started.

1

MY MOTIVATORS

There many motivators for having a good spending plan or budget in place. In this chapter, I describe four basic motivators to why a spending plan or budget is necessary. Any one of these motivators, alone, would suggest it's a good idea to have a spending plan in place! Every individual is different and will have different motives and goals. At the end, on the **"Before Proceeding"** page, you will write out your own personal motivators and goals.

The four categories of **Motivators** include:

- A Decent Retirement
- Spending Goals
- Eliminating Debt
- Emergency Savings

Most likely the goals that you come up with, fit into one of these four categories.

A DECENT RETIREMENT

The only sure way to build up savings for your retirement years is to invest regularly over a very long period of time. The only way to invest consistently is to have cash available at the end of each month. Being on a budget allows for cash to be freed up each month for investing, which can help you accomplish your retirement goal. Yes, the average person can perform "wealth building" techniques that will yield a decent retirement. Now, you won't become as "wealthy" in terms of monetary standards compared to mega- million dollar CEO's, but you can have a decent retirement, if you plan for one.

Let's look at wealth-building a little deeper. One thing we know for sure is that the stock market goes up and down erratically. The second thing we know is that it goes up consistently over very long periods of time, as can be seen on the chart on the next page. This chart from *StockCharts.com* shows the historical results of the *Dow Jones Industrial Average*. Note the peaks and valleys that can occur from year to year. You can also see the general upward trend. For almost any 20-year period, the trend is significantly upward.

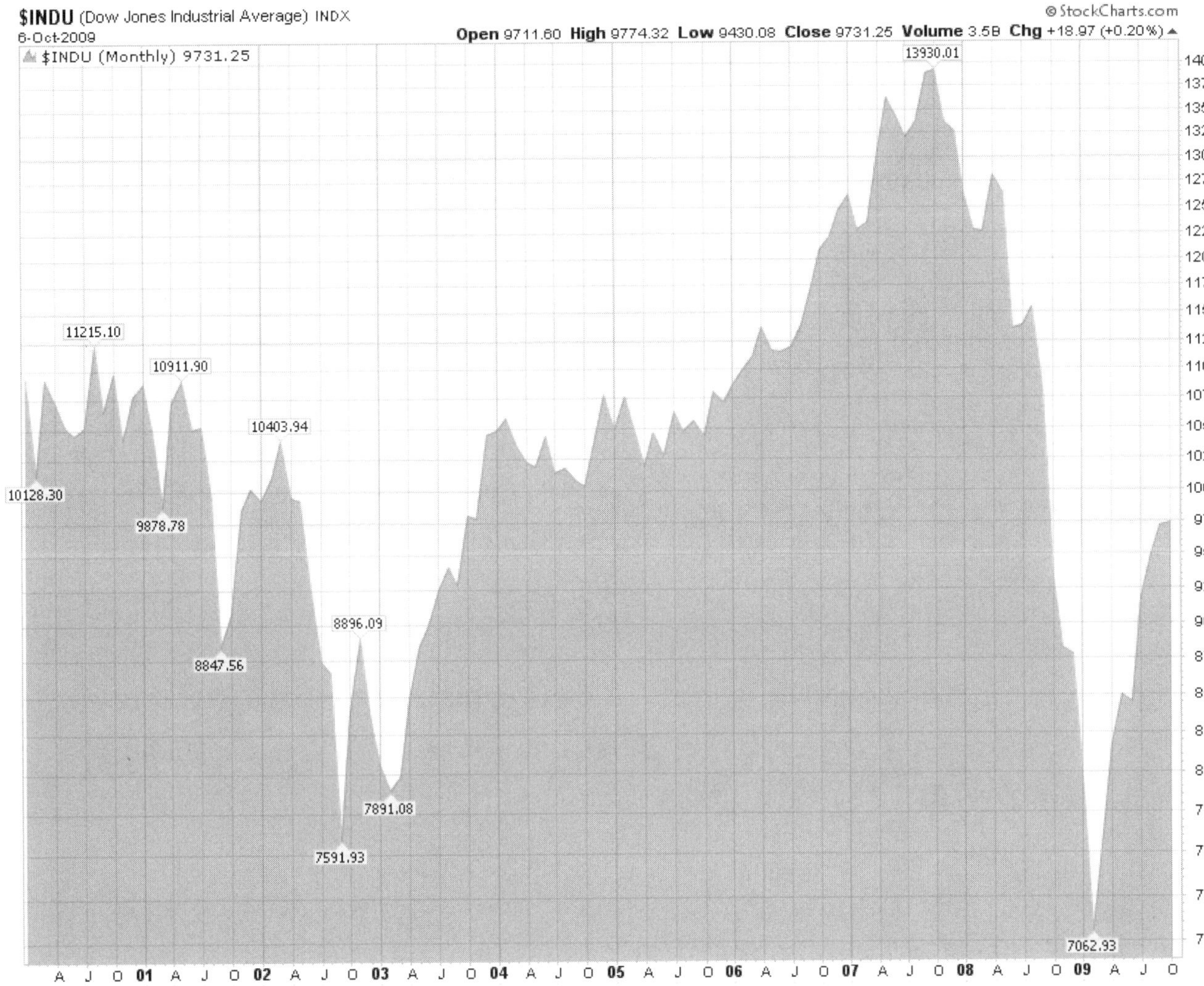

The chart clearly shows that an important ingredient to wealth-building is time. The second ingredient is to have cash available at the end of each month to invest, which the "Get a GRASP..." program will help you with. The third ingredient is how to invest it. I will not cover investing techniques in this workbook. I'll save that for the financial planners, or perhaps a later book. But I will give you a couple of specific examples of why budgeting and generating cash for investment on a consistent basis is so important.

It only takes a $100 or $200 per month to build a significant amount of money over a 20-year period. Of course, if you are young and have 40 years to invest, that's even better. Here are a couple examples I like to use:

- **Saving $100** per month for 20 years at 8% interest will yield $58,902
- **Increasing** that saving to $200 per month for 20 years would yield $117,804
- **A young couple** just starting out who save $100 per month for 40 years would have $349,100
- **If that same** young couple started out saving $200 per month for 40 years, they would have $698,201

That is the power of compounding interest. It doesn't matter at what age you start. Even if you're 50 years old, saving $100 or $200 a month will give you a nice chunk of change when you're 70.

You may have been told that you need millions of dollars to retire. That is simply not true. You would need millions of dollars to retire IF you want to live on 10% of the interest and keep the principal for beneficiaries or want to do a significant amount of world traveling and live lavishly, or just die rich. There's nothing wrong with any of those, but it's not necessary for a decent retirement. Many people retire just to slow down, enjoy their families, and travel occasionally. You can have a much smaller nest egg and retire just fine by allocating a little bit of your budget towards retirement.

My main purpose here is to show that:

- History has proven that significant growth occurs over time
- Investing a small amount per month can bring you significant results over time
- You can realize a retirement goal, if you plan for it
- You don't have to save millions of dollars to have a decent retirement

SPENDING GOALS

In addition to saving for a decent retirement, nearly everyone would like to have money for a vacation, new furniture, a reliable car, college education, charitable giving— just to name a few. How many times have you wished you had saved enough money to take vacation? The truth is it's hard to save without training and discipline.

Save up for such expenditures, the same way you would for retirement, by allocating a certain part of your budget each month. The only difference will be that rather than investing long term, you will be saving for the shorter term. For example, it might take only a few months to save for a new TV, but could take several years to save for a your son's or daughter's two year education at a community college. Rather than investing in the stock market with mutual funds, have a separate savings account at your bank, depending on the goal.

The key is to make a list of the expenditures (spending goals) you would like to make over the next year, three years, and five years. Then figure how much needs to be saved each month for those purchases. That may add up to a whole lot of money you currently don't have. Take that list and prioritize it. For now, your list may contain both "needs" and "wants." That is okay. In Chapter 2, I'll show you how to separate those out and prioritize in more detail.

By living within your means, eliminating your debt, and developing a responsible budget, you can have money available at the end of the month for investing or saving. By saving or investing on a regular basis, the examples given above could be a reality for you.

ELIMINATE DEBT

There's only one kind of debt: bad debt. Any debt that you have is setting you back from achieving your financial goals and, more importantly, true peace of mind. One of your highest priorities should be to pay off any non-mortgage debt.

Even mortgage debt, commonly considered a 'good' form of debt, is a bad thing for many people in this economy. Just ask anyone whose house is "under water," a term commonly used to describe a home whose value is less than their mortgage balance. If a need to sell that home should occur, not only is all the equity gone, but you will have to show up at the closing with a check for the difference of the mortgage balance minus the sold price. Mortgage companies are not forgiving organizations!

Based on these recent lessons-learned from today's economy, if you are looking for a home, it's wise to save up for at least a 20% down payment with a conventional fixed rate mortgage. It may take longer to get in the home you want, or you may have to scale back on your dream home, but having 20% of the purchase price as down payment will pay off in the long run.

Other than mortgage debt, many people have a significant amount of other debt in bank loans for cars, boats, home improvements, credit cards, etc. It should be common knowledge that you are paying significantly more for an item if you take out a loan or use a credit card.

Example: For a car purchased for $20,000 at 8% interest with $2,000 down for 4 years, your payment will be $439 per month and you will pay a total of $23,093 for the car. But here's the thing: you just spent $23K for a car that's now worth about $12,000.

I'm all for buying the car. Using the knowledge gained from this "Get a GRASP..." workbook you will learn the significance of saving up for an item and then making your purchase.

There are many resources available for why debt is a bad idea. The best resource I've seen is from the Dave Ramsey "Financial Peace" program. In that program Dave goes through example after example of why it's a good idea to avoid debt. He discusses the history of credit cards, the high pressure marketing campaigns from banks to use credit cards, and the ultimate rip-offs on consumers. A list of recommended works is in the Recommended Reading section in the Appendix.

Sometimes history and our elders are great teachers too. There is a lot of wisdom we can learn from and apply to today's environment. The best anti-debt story I've heard recently was from a good friend of mine, Dave Smith (a great Financial Coach, by the way), who recently shared a story about a friend:

"My oldest daughter and I had lunch the other day with a dear friend of mine I don't see as much as I'd like. We were talking and he shared his grandfather's view on credit cards. His Grandfather was of the depression era before they sold 'pets on payments'. His Grandfather described credit cards this way: "They are like setting bear traps all over your house then walking around in the dark."

That's a pretty good description of what having a whole bunch of debt can feel like! In this program you will learn a method to pay off this debt as quickly as possible. You'll be able to walk around your home freely, without the bear traps—or the bears!

EMERGENCY SAVINGS

In today's economic environment it is more critical than ever to have a personal financial plan and corresponding budget to avoid those life-crises such as a serious illness or unemployment. They can happen at any moment. If you are not prepared for such emergencies, you may experience financial hardship on top of the life-crisis. Having an appropriate spending plan and a budget will allow you to save in case such emergency occurs.

An example is the recent and unprecedented economic "perfect storm" of the housing crisis, banking crisis, automotive crisis, and resulting high levels of unemployment. Not since the Great Depression have we seen such economic turmoil. Even if you are not currently one of the unemployed, surely you know someone who has been devastated by the current downturn.

A previous rule of thumb was to have 3-6 months of living expenses saved up for such emergencies. Today's unemployed are looking at 1-2 years to get back on track with former income levels, if ever. Many are seeking lower income jobs just to get by, but in some regions, even those jobs are hard to come by. So I'm going to say that it's wise to have 12-18 months of living expenses saved in case any life-crisis should occur. Note that it's 12-18 months of living expenses, not 12-18 months of income. As you go through this workbook process, you will learn what living expenses are and, more importantly, how to manage them.

The eye-opener from this current recession, is that devastation can strike anyone at any time, and at any age. No longer are high salaried, white collar workers exempt from the chopping blocks of large financial institutions and manufacturing companies. Serious illness or unemployment can strike anyone at any time, any industry, any geographic, any demographic.

A good spending plan or budget will enable you to put a little bit of money away each month, into a savings account to be used in case such life-crises occur.

JUST DO IT!

All it takes to save for retirement and emergencies, set spending goals and eliminate debt is an understanding of a budget process and a commitment to follow through. Once you put this budget plan in place, it won't be long before you can begin to see progress on short term goals. Before you know it, you'll be sitting down with a financial planner for assistance with investment options for meeting long term goals, such as retirement.

Studies have shown that if you learn a new technique or acquire a new idea, it must be implemented within 24 hours or it will probably get lost. So take each chapter to heart, answer the "Before Proceeding" questions when prompted, and your plan will start to unfold right before you.

It all starts with a plan. Just do it! The next chapter will help you with some key decisions to help get the plan started.

BEFORE PROCEEDING

What are your personal key motivators for starting a budgeting process?

List at least three specific financial goals including amount of item and priority.

NOTES

2

MY DECISIONS

In Chapter 1, you established your motivators and financial goals. Chapter 2 of our "Motivation" theme is to make some key decisions that will keep you motivated throughout the spending plan and budgeting process. Creating a spending plan and budget is hard only if you don't have the motivators, goals and key decisions in place.

The motivators, goals and key decisions will be the foundation upon which you build your spending plan and budget.

The four basic up-front decisions that will keep you motivated throughout the process are:

- Decision to get started, wherever you are
- Commit to learning the process
- Distinguish between your needs and wants
- Live within your means

By making these key decisions and then applying the knowledge provided in this workbook, I believe you can create a workable budget within a couple of months. The most difficult part is to make the decision to get started. I will start with that and then walk you through each of the other decisions...

1ST DECISION:
GET STARTED, WHEREVER YOU ARE

As I mentioned in the previous chapter, if you learn a new technique or acquire a new idea, it must be implemented within 24 hours or it will probably get lost or forgotten. The fact that you invested in this workbook is a good indication that you are at least curious about your financial situation. Now, make the decision to get started, wherever you are in your life, no matter what your age or life circumstance.

Take a look again at the example in the previous chapter for a 50-year old that saves $200 for 20 years at 8%. At age 70, there's a nice chunk of change to live on for the next 20 years. With a healthy lifestyle, you could easily live to 90 or more. It will be really nice to have that extra money during years 70 through 90! So, if you're 50, just start where you are. You do not have to be young to have financial goals.

You may be thinking that age isn't your only impediment. Perhaps you feel like life has given you a bum rap you cannot overcome. Maybe you had one of those life-crises and have been set back financially because of it. These things do happen, but we can still make the decision to move forward by "Starting Where You Are."

I'd like to share the inspirational story of Chris Gardner, whom, as you may know, was the author of *"Pursuit of Happyness"* which became a movie starring Will Smith. The true story and movie is one of a single and homeless father with a very young child (age five in the movie, but actually 14 months at the time of the story). In the movie, Will Smith overcomes very difficult circumstances to achieve great success as a stock broker and ultimately, his own stock brokerage firm. He overcame the most difficult of circumstances to achieve success.

In the new book, **"Start Where You Are,"** Chris Gardner writes about life lessons for overcoming the most difficult life circumstances. The book is packed with 44 life lessons to help you get from where you are to where you want to be. Simply start where you are and go from there. I highly recommend this book for anyone that feels disadvantaged, too old, not smart enough, without choices, or without resources.

We all have personal circumstances to overcome in different areas of our lives. But in order to achieve our goals, we need to start somewhere. For financial goals, this **"Get a GRASP..."** workbook is designed to help you get there, no matter you're age, life circumstance, or financial situation. The more you know about where you are and where you want to be, the better you can avoid financial setbacks.

Make the commitment that developing a spending plan and budget is important, and to begin right away, no matter the circumstance. Doing so will enable you to take a giant leap forward to gain control of your financial future and achieve your goals.

2ND DECISION:
COMMIT TO LEARNING A BUDGETING PROCESS

Once you've decided to "Start Where You Are," the next most important decision is to commit to learning the budgeting process outlined in Part 2: Knowledge. In that part of the workbook I walk you through the techniques and steps related to each of the budgeting forms. Each of the budgeting steps has related forms to fill out information. At the end of each chapter I provide a set of questions to make sure you are on track before proceeding to the next step.

The **"Get a GRASP..."** process is the five-step budgeting process. Each of the five letters of the word GRASP equates to a step in the budgeting process:

Gather all your financial data
Record
Analyze
Set Up Budget and Accounts
Pay Off Debt

This is the simplest and most logical approach available to develop a spending plan and budget. By learning this process you will be able to see your financial situation by glancing at just a few charts. You will also be able to see how to get to your goals.

Your second decision is to make a commitment to understand and apply a budgeting process.

3RD DECISION:
DISTINGUISH BETWEEN YOUR "NEEDS" AND "WANTS"

Sometimes it's difficult to realize that what we need is more important than what we want. You may want a vacation, but if the roof is in need of repair, you may have to forego the vacation for a year or so. It's important to distinguish between "needs" and "wants" when creating your spending plan. I'm a strong proponent for spending on the "wants" and enjoying life to the fullest. But it's imperative to know and address the "needs" so that you are not living in a home with a leaky roof.

Once you learn how to develop an appropriate spending plan and budget, it will be much easier to see where your money is, and what it will take to save up for some of your short term goals. Depending on your circumstances, you may have to temporarily trim "wants" in order to shift money to your "needs" and then to long term financial goals.

In the "Before Proceeding" section at the end of this chapter, I ask you to take your financial goals from Chapter 1 and rewrite them into two categories: Needs and Wants.

Later, when you develop your spending plan, depending on your circumstances, it may be necessary to trim some of the "wants."

The third decision is to make a commitment to prioritize your "needs" and "wants" and to make adjustments, if necessary, to meet your financial goals.

4TH DECISION:
LIVE WITHIN YOUR MEANS

As with any worthwhile plan, you not only need to decide to get started and learn as much as you can, you also need to decide to "do whatever it takes" to accomplish your goals. In the case of developing your budget and meeting financial goals, it may mean making some sacrifices to get your spending in line with your income.

In some cases, a lot of cases actually, people are living on credit cards to meet what they think are their basic needs. That is a recipe for financial disaster. Dave Ramsey has a great line in his Financial Peace program and on many billboards: "Act Your Wage." This is so true!

Depending on your current financial circumstances, getting your spending in line with your income could be painful. Doing whatever it takes may mean any one or some combination of the following:

- Eliminate credit card spending *(if you use credit cards)*
- Paying off debt
- Cutting back on discretionary spending such as eating out
- Curtailing spending on kid's toys or entertainment
- Other cuts in discretionary spending such as mobile phone, cable TV, etc.

Those are just a few examples of what types of spending cuts can be made to bring your spending in line with income level and how much needs to be saved to reach monthly goals. There are other ideas for trimming your budget in the article, "*101 Ways to Trim*

Your Budget" which can be accessed via the internet at -

http://www.careonecredit.com/Knowledge/101WaystoTrimYourBudget.aspx
Other resources are also listed in the *Appendix*.

If you have cut your budget to the bone, still have a lot of debt to pay off, and can't realize a spending plan to meet your financial goals, another solution is to raise your household income. Some possible options include:

- Perhaps another household member could take a temporary part time job

- A college student could pick up part of their own expenses, hence freeing up some of your money

- You may need to pick up a temporary part time job, just long enough for you to catch up on eliminating some or all of your debt

- Raise money through a garage sale

- Sell a car for a much cheaper one

- Move into less expensive living arrangements

Trimming expenses to the bone and extra part time work are all options, if you have been living beyond your means. But once you get past those issues and start to realize your financial goals, you will never return to the old way of doing things!

The fourth critical decision is to commit to doing whatever it takes to live within your means.

BEFORE PROCEEDING

I have made the decision to start where I'm at, whether I'm 20 or 50, whether I'm in debt or not, and no matter what my educational background may be

Yes _____No ______

I have made the decision to learn and apply the 5-Step "Get a GRASP..." process

Yes _____No ______

Rewrite your financial goals in terms of "Needs" and "Wants"

NEEDS	WANTS
______________________________	______________________________
______________________________	______________________________
______________________________	______________________________
______________________________	______________________________
______________________________	______________________________

I have made the decision to do whatever it takes to live within my means, pay off debt, and cut discretionary spending to generate extra cash at the end of the month to apply to my goals

Yes _____No ______

NOTES

3
GETTING STARTED

My goal with **"Get a GRASP..."** is to make it as easy as possible to achieve your goals with a simple process. Each chapter walks you through how to organize your financial information and record it on the budgeting forms provided in the Appendix.

After each chapter is between 2 and 5 questions. By answering those questions, you are applying the knowledge gained from the chapter to your personal situation. Doing so will prepare you for the next chapter. It is designed to be as easy as possible, yet properly prepare you for the next step.

MAKE IT FUN!

This workbook is designed to be a hands-on approach to helping organize and analyze your personal financial situation. For first-time use, I recommend setting aside a couple of hours, a clear desk, a quiet environment, and your spouse or significant other at your side. Learning as a team will be beneficial and can ease the pain of doing something most of us dread. Make it a fun, learning, fun, bonding, and fun experience! Did I mention to make it fun?

Don't attempt to do all the steps in one sitting. I broke the process into five logical steps so that you can spend quality time on each step before proceeding to the next step. Your finances didn't get messed up in one night, so don't expect to fix everything by burning the midnight oil. Take your time. Your budget will not be perfect the first time. Fully expect to make tweaks from month to month for the first few months. It takes at least 90 days to nail it down. So take your time and have fun with it!

Part of the fun is establishing your motivations. In other words, establish why setting up a budget is important to you. Is it so that you can have extra money to: begin an emergency fund? Take a vacation? Build wealth? Give more to charity? Establishing one or more motivations will keep the budgeting process fun, as you will see results every month going towards your goal(s). Make sure you have completed Chapter 1!

TEAM PARTICIPATION

Your success depends highly on involving your spouse or significant other in the process from start to finish. Unless each of you participate, agree on your goals and objectives, and make a commitment to make this work, it probably won't. It's not unusual for one partner to have vastly different ideas about spending, saving or budgeting than the other... all the more reason to get on the same page! Going through this process will help you communicate and understand each other's position much better.

In Chapter 1, you made a list of your financial goals. Compare your list with that of your partner. You will learn a lot about each other! If one partner is a spender and the other a saver, there will be some fruitful discussions! But it's important to have this discussion, compromise, and establish one prioritized list of goals. This combined list of motivators and goals will now be the starting point for you and your partner.

Later, in the "Set Up Budget and Accounts" chapter, this idea of teamwork and compromise will come into play again. In that step, there will need to be a meeting of the minds agreement on various categories of the budget (e.g. monthly spending on food, clothing, or entertainment) that often have varying levels of importance, depending on the individual.

For now, it is important to come to team agreement and to set a stake in the ground on motivators and goals for each person. Keep in mind these goals and motivators change as life circumstances can change over time.

WHICH VERSION SHOULD I USE?

Now is the time to decide whether to use the hardcopy form approach or the MS Excel spreadsheet version. Blank hardcopy forms are in Appendix A. Print out as many copies as needed. An example of an MS Excel version with fabricated data can be found in Appendix B.

The hardcopy forms are very useful if any one of the following conditions exist:

- You are not comfortable using a computer
- You do not have MS Excel installed
- You have MS Excel installed on your computer but it's too intimidating for you
- You prefer to do the math yourself

The MS Excel spreadsheet version is available for purchase from the website at http://PersonalEconomicCoachingLive.com. Please note that the MS Excel spreadsheet version has several advantages not available on the hardcopy forms:

Easy data input with color coded "cells"

- Calculations are made by the computer quickly and accurately
- Pie charts of key financial information are generated automatically
- Monthly changes are a snap by just editing the previous month's data

If you choose to use the MS Excel spreadsheet version, you must have MS Excel 2003 or later installed on your computer. Please verify that you have MS Excel program installed on your computer before you download the budgeting spreadsheets from the website mentioned above.

STEP ZERO

The best way to start is to have this workbook, the blank budgeting forms, and the example spreadsheet forms printed out and readily available for reference. See the Appendix for the related forms. Have a couple of hours of uninterrupted time set aside for each step with your partner and you are ready to begin!

QUICK SUMMARY OF STEPS 1-5

Step 1 GATHER INFORMATION

(30 minutes - 2 hours, one time only)

Once you have your work environment set up you are ready for Step 1: GATHER your data. For most people, this will take some time to find all the relative statements of income, assets, and debts. Step 1 is gathering up all of that information and can take anywhere between 30 minutes to 2 hours depending how organized your paper files are.

Step 2 RECORD INFORMATION

(1 - 2 hours first month, significantly less thereafter)

This is the step for recording the data that you gathered from Step 1 into either the hardcopy forms or the MS Excel spreadsheet. If you are using the hardcopy forms in the Appendix, it is best to start with the first budgeting form and proceed in order until you've completed all the forms. If you are using the MS Excel spreadsheet, simply follow the forms in order as calculations occur, proceeding through the tabs (forms) to input data.

Step 3

ANALYZE (30 minutes - 1 hour)
Now we determine if you have any cash left over at the end of the month! The challenge is to set a realistic budget so that you do have cash at the end of the month for saving, investing, or putting to some other financial goal. This is where the rubber meets the road.

Step 4

SET UP BUDGET AND ACCOUNTS (1 - 2 hours)
This step helps you set up your bill pay accounts through your bank. By setting up automatic payments you save time and increase the accuracy and timeliness of the payments. There is a chapter on electronic banking later on that demystifies the whole world of electronic banking. You'll benefit greatly by implementing an automated payment schedule!

Step 5

PAY OFF DEBT (30 minutes - 1 hour)
It takes about 30-60 minutes to figure which strategy will pay down debt as quickly as possible. I'll show you the process of paying off the smallest debt first, which is the fastest approach. This is the exciting part - watching your debt diminish month after month!

AVAILABLE HELP

Help is available. Should you have any questions, I invite you to visit my website at http://PersonalEconomicCoachingLive.com. You can Email me from the "contact us" tab. I will either answer your question via email or refer you to a Financial Coach. One-on-one coaching, if required, is available for a fee. Simply click the "Coaching Services" tab on the website above and you will see a list of coaching services available.

BEFORE PROCEEDING

My partner is actively engaged in this process with me:

Yes ______No _______

We have an agreed upon list of motivators and goals and prioritized our list of "needs" and "wants":

Yes ______No _______

I have selected the budgeting form version that I will use:

_______Hardcopy

_______MS Excel spreadsheet

________I have the MS Excel program installed on my computer

________I have purchased and downloaded the budgeting spreadsheets

________I have the blank budgeting forms printed out for reference

I will allocate at least the minimum amount of time for each of the steps:

Yes ______No _______

PART II
KNOWLEDGE

BUDGETING PROCESS AND TOOLS

"The secret of getting ahead is getting started. The secret of getting started is breaking your complex overwhelming tasks into small manageable tasks, and then starting on the first one."
- Mark Twain -

The next six chapters deal with the actual budgeting process and provide you with the knowledge to create a personal customized *Spending Plan or Budget.* The overall budgeting process can be rather overwhelming if you have never done it before. Therefore, I break it down into "small manageable tasks," so that you will have meaningful results starting with the very first step.

This next section will involve some work on your part. You have the choice of using the blank hardcopy forms or the MS Excel computer spreadsheet. As you walk through all the logical steps and gain the knowledge to utilize your tool of choice, you will effectively put together your monthly spending plan and budget to meet your financial goals.

NOTES

4
STEP ONE
GATHER INFORMATION

The very first step is to gather and organize all your information including assets, debts, income, and monthly expenses. These can be pulled from your monthly statements, check book, credit card bills, invoices, etc. It is an essential first step to get your arms around the money coming in and how it is being spent.

Gathering up all of this information may be enlightening! You will physically see the stack of bills being paid each month. Sometimes that can be overwhelming, which may be why you've avoided coming up with a spending plan or budget in the past. But don't let the amount of information scare you. Once you gather up the information, I'll show you how to organize it on the budget forms and you will be able to see how all of the financial information comes together on a few simple charts.

Once you find all the statements, I recommend organizing them into separate piles or folders labeled:

- Assets
- Debts
- Net Income
- Fixed Monthly Expenses
- Variable Monthly Expenses

Once you have gathered up all the information and statements, it is time to proceed to Step 2.

DEFINITIONS FOR THIS STEP

Assets are owned items, such as personal property, house, car, and other significant items of value.

Debts are items in your possession but you owe money to an institution or individual. (Note: house is probably an asset and a debt. I will cover how to handle that in the next chapter.) A debt could also be services rendered but not yet paid for such as medical bills.

Net Income is any source of money coming in either through paycheck, unemployment, alimony, child support, or any investments, after taxes have been withdrawn

Fixed monthly expenses recur monthly and the payment does not change. For example, rent or mortgage payments are a fixed monthly expense. A car payment is another example.

Variable monthly expenses would recur monthly but the amount changes. Examples are utility bills, food, clothing, etc.

BUDGETING FORMS REFERENCED

This is only the information gathering step, so you do not need to fill in any of the budgeting forms in the Appendix. However, when gathering income and monthly expenses it may be helpful to look at these forms to see if there are any items or categories you may have forgotten.

BEFORE PROCEEDING

I have five piles (or five folders) of statements, one for each: Assets, Debts, Income, Fixed Expenses, and Variable Expenses

Yes ______No _______

I have looked at the reference categories on all the forms and I have found all the statements and information that pertain to me

Yes ______No _______

NOTES

5

STEP TWO RECORD INFORMATION

The second step is recording the information you gathered in such a format that it can easily be tracked monthly.

Before proceeding with this step, you should have made a decision on which version to use: either the hardcopy form version or the MS Excel computer spreadsheet. For more information, please review the section in Chapter 3: Getting Started.

The hardcopy forms in the Appendix are fine if you don't have access to MS Excel on your computer. The advantage of the MS Excel spreadsheets is ease of data entry, automatic calculations of the financial data and the generation of pie charts to easily see data relationships.

I've designed the forms with a color coding scheme to make it as easy as possible. The lightly-shaded areas are the only place you will need to enter information. The blue-colored areas are headings and are non-editable on the spreadsheet version.

Now let's discuss the process of recording data on each of the separate forms provided.

ASSET FORM

For each asset category, enter in a description of the asset. For example, the Primary Residence category could simply be your home address. Next, enter the financial institution name and account number if you currently owe money on that asset. Lastly, in the right-most column, enter the total Asset value (what you would get if you were to sell the asset on the open market).

Repeat the process above for each asset. Once all the assets are listed, add up the right column for the total value of all your assets. On the spreadsheet version, the total value of the assets will automatically be calculated. This chart provides a detailed view of each asset.

In the second table on the asset form, add up all the assets that are Residences and put that number into the lightly-shaded column. Add up all the assets that are Vehicles and put that number into the lightly-shaded column. Repeat for the other asset types. This chart gives a good view of each asset by type.

DEBT FORM

We will follow a similar approach for this form as we did on the asset form, except there will be a bit more information we need to capture.

For each debt category, enter a description of the debt. For example, the Primary Residence category could simply be your home address. Next, enter the financial institution name and account number if money is owed on that asset. If you have the spreadsheet version, these fields will be filled in automatically for you based on your input on the Asset form.

In the "Amount Owed and Mo Pymt" columns, enter the amount owed and the monthly payment for each of the debt items. If any debt categories don't apply to you, simply leave those cells blank.

Then in the right-most column enter the length or "Term" and Interest Rate (yearly) for each of the debts. These last two columns are optional, but recommended if you have the information.

Repeat the process above for each of the assets that you have gathered in your asset pile or folder. Once all the assets are listed, add up the right column for a total value of all your assets. On the spreadsheet version, the total value of the assets is automatically calculated.

MONTHLY INCOME FORM

On this form simply find the income categories that pertain to you and enter the net monthly amount from each source. Net refers to the actual amount you receive after taxes have been taken out.

In the next chart on this same form, it asks you to enter your weekly net amounts from all the sources that pertain to you. You will need this net weekly amount when you figure your budget.

The totals in the individual green cells should be exactly the same.

In the Debt/Income Ratio section, two figures are calculated that are valuable to financial institutions when applying for a loan. The first is Debt to Net Income. To get this number, take your monthly debt payments from the previous Debt Form and divide that by your Net Income (the number in the green cell on this form). The result will be a fraction.

The next calculation on this form is the Mortgage Debt to Net Income. To calculate this number, take only your Mortgage payments from the previous Debt Form and divide that by your Net Income (the number in the green cell on this form). The result will also be a fraction.

On the hardcopy forms you will need to do the math yourself; the MS Excel spreadsheet version automatically calculates the ratios.

MONTHLY EXPENSES FORM

On this form, enter both the fixed monthly expenses and the variable monthly expenses. From all the monthly expense data you've gathered, enter either the monthly amount or the yearly amount. For example, figure Property Taxes, by adding the biannual payments and entering the total into the lightly-shaded Yearly Amt column.

You may have to get creative on allocating certain monthly expenses to the pre-defined categories provided. That's okay; just make sure you have accounted for all of your expenses.

For any category that has a yearly expense only, divide that number by 12 and enter it in the Mo Amount column. Then add up all the numbers in the Mo Amount column to get your Total Expenses per Month. Again, the spreadsheet version will do this automatically.

Make sure all of your monthly expenses are accurately recorded on this form and you're ready for the next step!

DEFINITIONS FOR THIS STEP

Hardcopy refers to a page that has been printed out, such as the hardcopy forms in Appendix A.

Spreadsheet refers to the computerized version of the hardcopy forms. The spreadsheet forms that I offer are based on MS Excel 2003, which you must have installed on your computer. Spreadsheet forms have many advantages over the hardcopy versions, as I mention throughout this workbook.

BUDGETING FORMS REFERENCED

- Asset form
- Debt form
- Net Income form
- Monthly Expenses form

BEFORE PROCEEDING

I have all of my assets listed on the Asset form

Yes ______No ______

I have all of my debts listed on the Debt form

Yes ______No ______

I have all of my net income listed on the Net Income form

Yes ______No ______

I have all of my monthly expenses listed on the Monthly Expenses form

Yes ______No______

6

STEP THREE ANALYZE

MS EXCEL SPREADSHEET USERS

This is the fun part if you're using the spreadsheet version. All you have to do is look at the Cash Flow Analysis form. Everything has been calculated out for you. You can see your spending analysis by category, including how far off you are from the general guideline. You can also see your Income vs. Spending Analysis calculated out for you. If the "delta," or difference, is a positive number, you are spending less than you are taking in and that is a positive sign. If the "delta" is negative, you are spending more than you bring in, and immediate action is required. You will need to trim back your discretionary spending so that total spending does not exceed your net monthly income.

Spreadsheet users may skip this next section.

HARDCOPY FORM USERS

If you are using the hardcopy forms, we have more work to do to complete the Cash Flow Analysis form. To get the Subtotal by Category number you will need to add up each component from the previous Monthly Expenses form.

For example, to get the number for the Charities category, go back to the Monthly Expenses form and add up all the line items you entered for Charities. That amount will go into the Subtotal by Category column for the Charities category on this form. Do that for each Category.

Next we're going to take each of these entries and divide by your Net Monthly Income to get the percentage of Total Net Monthly Income. As a reminder, your Net Monthly Income is the green highlighted cell on the Monthly Income form.

You should now have numbers in all columns except the Delta from the Guideline column. We are ready to calculate that now. For each of the Categories, simply subtract your percentage of Total Net Monthly Income from the General Guideline percentage column and enter the delta in the lightly-shaded cell.

You now have a clear picture of your spending habits by category and can see how it compares to a general guideline.

The next chart on this form is the ***Income vs. Spending Analysis*** which is

Total Net Monthly Income -Total Expenses Per Month

If the number is positive, that is encouraging. If it's negative, you will need to make some adjustments, either by increasing income or reducing expenses.

WHAT IF MY CASH FLOW IS NEGATIVE?

Paying off debt will be very difficult with a negative cash flow. Start by reducing or eliminating all discretionary spending which includes, but not limited to:

- Restaurants
- Movies out
- Other entertainment
- Eliminate or reduce other services such as cable TV and mobile phone plans

After you do all of that, rerun the numbers. If you still have a negative cash flow, keep cutting expenses further. There's an article entitled *"101 Ways to Trim Your Budget"* at http://www.careonecredit.com/Knowledge./101WaystoTrimYourBudget.aspx
Use that as a source for even more ideas.

If you are still at negative cash flow after all of that, consider working overtime, if available, or perhaps finding a temporary part time job until you can catch up on the expenses and get back to neutral or positive cash flow.

These are not easy steps and will require sacrifice and commitment on your part. This is when those "motivators" come in handy. Remember that it's the end result that you're shooting for. Some give-and-take along the way should be expected.

IS IT GOOD TO HAVE POSITIVE CASH FLOW?

Yes, but it still needs to be dealt with. If you have positive cash flow and have debt, you are missing an opportunity to pay off that debt quickly. Apply any extra cash to outstanding debts. I will discuss how to pay off debt quickly in *Chapter 8*.

If you have positive cash flow and no debt, that is really good. But if you don't have a plan on how to wisely spend or invest the extra cash, chances are you are still missing an opportunity to reach your financial goals faster. You are probably spending a lot on discretionary spending that could be channeled to much more productive uses.

The bottom line is that you should target any extra cash at the end of every month to either paying down debt or toward achieving your financial goals.

WHEN BEING A "NET-ZERO" IS A GOOD THING

Now, most people will do anything to avoid being labeled a 'zero' in any aspect of their life. But in the case of your monthly cash flow, I think you can see the objective of getting to 'net-zero' is actually a good thing. It means that you are cognizant of your financial situation AND have intelligently figured out where to spend or invest any extra cash. In essence, your cash flow is "net-zero."

If you can follow the logic in this chapter, you should be able to get to "net-zero" on your cash flow in relatively short order. It may take a couple months with some give-and-take on the discretionary spending and how much extra you put into paying down debt or toward your financial goals, but you will get to "net-zero." Just be patient and have some fun playing with the many scenarios that are available. The MS Excel spreadsheet is extremely helpful in analyzing different scenarios "on-the-fly."

DEFINITIONS FOR THIS STEP

Cash flow refers to the money coming in every month from the various income sources MINUS the monthly expenses.

Delta in this context refers to the difference between two numbers.

Net-Zero is a term I use in the context of Cash Flow Analysis to mean all the money going out equals the amount coming in.

BUDGETING FORMS REFERENCED

- Cash Flow Analysis form
- Monthly Expenses form (Hardcopy form users will use this as a reference)

BEFORE PROCEEDING

I have analyzed my monthly Cash Flow:
Yes ______No _______

If NEGATIVE cash flow, I will take the following actions to reduce my discretionary spending *(see Chapter 2 and Resources in Appendix):*

1) ____

2) ____

3) ____

If POSITIVE cash flow, I have identified the following financial goals to which I will increase saving or investments:

1) ____

2) ____

3) ____

I am now operating at a net-zero Cash Flow:
Yes ______No _______

NOTES

7

ELECTRONIC BANKING

Before we move on to Step 4: Set Up Budget and Accounts, it's worthwhile to review the topic of electronic banking. Many people are comfortable with this new technology and others are not. If you are already comfortable with electronic banking, have monthly payees established and know the difference between an Auto Pay and an eCheck, then feel free to move on to the next chapter.

If electronic banking seems a bit daunting and some of the terms unfamiliar, then this chapter can help ease the transition to the world of electronic banking. You will need access to a computer at home and use a financial institution that has free web banking capabilities, as most do. I do not recommend doing electronic banking from public computers, such as public libraries. The technology most likely is safe, but prying eyeballs all around you is cause for concern.

WHY ELECTRONIC BANKING?

There are five big reasons to consider electronic banking:

1. Once it's set up, it will save time
2. For fixed repeating payments (such as mortgage, car payment, etc.) it is extremely accurate in paying these bills monthly
3. It can save money, approximately $3-$4 per month in stamps depending on how many payments you mail out every month
4. It provides the discipline to manage monthly expenditures
5. It's a lot more fun than writing checks!

Check out your banking institution's website for how to sign-up. If your bank doesn't have free web banking, I would seriously consider searching for another institution.

When selecting a bank or credit union, ask about setting up "sub-accounts." We'll discuss this in the next chapter, but basically it's multiple savings accounts linked to one checking account. This feature makes it easier to set up savings for specific future items, such as yearly payments (home insurance) or other financial goal (vacation). If you can't find any financial institution in your area that offers "sub-accounts," you can still proceed with a single savings account. More on all of that later.

COMMON MYTHS

There may still be some myths out there even though electronic banking has been around for years. I'll go through each one quickly and simply to put your mind at ease.

■ **Myth 1** Electronic Banking Isn't Secure

Computers in general are very safe as long as your home system is secure and you have the all the recommended passwords in place. As I mentioned earlier, I do not recommend performing electronic banking from a public computer. In the same way that you protect your PIN number when entered at a merchant's checkout, your electronic banking should be protected from any prying eyes. Your banking session will generally be from 5 to 15 minutes and that is just too long to keep your screen protected. Use a computer from your home.

Also, most financial institutions today have strict security processes in place for their online clients, including multi-layered passwords. They also typically deploy the latest SSL technology (Security Socket Layer). I won't get into the technical details, but basically anything transferred over an SSL network is encrypted for your protection. Check with your financial institution for any questions or concerns.

You should not have any security issues if you use a home computer, keep passwords and security in place, and use a reputable financial institution with an additional layer of passwords and SSL.

■ **Myth 2** Electronic Banking is Hard to Learn

There is some learning curve to using a computer for electronic banking, but it is not hard. Most people can learn on their own, but even if you struggle a bit, there is help available. Most financial institutions are more than happy to help you get your accounts set up. Many have a help line that you can call while also offering online assistance via a little help "window" that allows you to "chat" with their help personnel by sending text messages back and forth.

■ **Myth 3** Electronic Banking Costs Too Much

Most financial institutions offer electronic banking for no charge. If your financial institution isn't one of them, consider switching to another one! There's probably a dozen in your neighborhood that offer it for free.

■ **MYTH 4** I DON'T NEED ELECTRONIC BANKING BECAUSE MY MERCHANTS OFFER "AUTO PAY"

Many merchants and utility companies offer "Auto Pay" service in which they debit your checking account each month for the amount of the bill. Please do not sign up for "Auto Pay" if your merchants offer this service! You are authorizing a third-party organization to have access to your checking account!

Your checking account is sacred ground because YOU are responsible to make sure all your bills can get paid from that account each month. Having an error by a merchant's "Auto Pay" could risk overdrawing the account.

For example, let's say your phone bill has an error and it's $200 higher than normal. There is a strong chance your phone company will deduct the higher amount from your checking account, before you have time to reconcile the issue with them. That's critical because you may not have that extra $200 to accommodate that higher charge. Unless you are keeping a sharp eye on things daily, you are exposing yourself to overdrawing your checking account for that month. I don't think it's wise to risk being late with your mortgage payment because of an error by another merchant's "Auto Pay."

Electronic banking overcomes this myth because it puts you in charge of paying your bills, you reconcile any issues before you pay, and concerns over third-party access to your checking account are eliminated. You will set up your own "Auto Pay" through your bank and YOU are in control, not the merchant.

In the next chapter I will show you how to set up your electronic bill paying through your financial institution's electronic banking system. This will put you in charge of paying your bills and help you budget. Read on to see how!

BEFORE PROCEEDING

I am convinced that electronic banking is safe and reliable:

Yes ______No _______

I have found a financial institution that will allow multiple savings accounts or "sub-accounts":

Yes ______ Name ______________________________________

No _______

I have registered with my financial institution for their web or electronic banking capabilities:

Yes ______No _______

NOTES

8

STEP FOUR SET UP BUDGET & ACCOUNTS

Now that you have analyzed your cash flow and registered for electronic banking, you are ready to take the next big step: Setting up your budget and electronic accounts. From *Chapter 5*, you have an intelligent idea of how much money is coming in and where it's going. From *Chapter 6*, you have all the myths of electronic banking debunked.

The next step is to set up your budget based on when you get paid so bills get paid on time and you don't run out of cash in between paychecks.

First, I will show you how to do that via the **Budget Plan** form and then will explain how you can set up the electronic accounts. You will develop the budget first, so you can see on paper (or computer screen) how your spending will occur for the month. It is much easier to make adjustments on paper prior to the actual spending. This is the essence of budgeting: To determine, in advance, how you will spend your available money for the month.

THE BUDGET PLAN FORM

This is a key form because, as I mentioned above, the essence of budgeting is to "see in advance" where your money is going for the month. Take a look at the Budget Plan form. You will see all the same categories that you've entered previously. Now you will be "budgeting on paper" (or on your computer screen) to pay these bills based on due date and pay day (hence the reason for putting in **Net Income** by week on the **Net Income** form).

For each category, take a look at when the bill comes due and "schedule" a payment. You do this by writing in, or keying in, the amount due and allocate it to one of the 4 or 5 weeks of the month (some months have 5 weeks). Repeat that process for each of the categories.

Over to the right on the **Budget Plan** form there is a *Payment Method* column. This is the suggested payment method you should set up for each of the category payments. The form also contains the definitions for each of these Payment Methods.

This form is extremely useful to make sure you have enough money available, by week, to pay the bills you are expected to pay. It is also very convenient to have this printed out before you go online to schedule your payments via your financial institution's web payment system.

If you are using the MS Excel spreadsheet version, follow the instructions in the spreadsheet, entering data in the lightly-shaded cells. Save the file with a file name that contains the date, e.g. name_ budget_30 aug 08. It's important to have the date as part of the file name, as you will see later on.

Next, let's set up your electronic accounts.

SET UP ACCOUNTS

This is probably the coolest part of the program because it's so unique. You'll be able to 'one up' all of your friends that are on a cash envelope plan, multiple bank plan, or no plan. It is essentially setting up two types of accounts through your financial institution:

- Saving accounts or sub-accounts
- Payee accounts

The combination of these two type of accounts will set up your electronic banking strategy and become a part of your monthly discipline, a key ingredient to budgeting. Setting up electronic checking and savings accounts can also provide time savings, accuracy, and discipline. Each of these type of accounts can easily be set up through your financial institution's online banking website.

As I mentioned at length in the previous chapter, many financial institutions now provide very secure web access so that you can set up these accounts and conduct transactions online very safely, with YOU in control of who gets paid and when. Again, I do not recommend giving your creditors the ability to access your account to extract the payment each month. It just doesn't make sense to give someone that access when you can easily control it yourself through your financial institution.

SAVING ACCOUNTS OR SUB-ACCOUNTS

The essence of this step is to set up a saving account system with your bank to electronically save and pay bills based on category. The concept works like this: You set up a savings account at a bank that allows for "sub-accounts." A sub-account is just another account under the main savings account that allows you to allocate savings for a specific category. Some financial institutions may allow you to designate the sub-account with a unique name.

For example, at my credit union I have a savings account and underneath I have sub-accounts named as follows:

- Real Estate Taxes
- Car Repairs
- Home Repairs
- Vacation
- Big Item Purchase

These are the categories I have that are for variable expenses. Your sub-categories may be different, but I think you get the idea that you now have a clear mechanism to save for those large variable expenses. I take the yearly costs for each of the items above, divide by 12, which is the monthly amount that needs to be transferred into each of the sub-accounts. When a bill comes due, such as real estate taxes, simply transfer the funds into your checking account and initiate an electronic payment.

Big Item Purchase can be anything on your wish list such as a new HDTV or furniture. Yep, no need to buy on impulse or credit card. Establish your goal, set up a savings sub-account, deposit monthly, and when you have the cash - BUY IT...and enjoy it without any payments!

You can set up as many sub-accounts as your banking institution will allow. It's an excellent way to save for the irregular/variable bills or savings goals that you've set.

PAYEE ACCOUNTS

Payee accounts are those merchants, utility companies, and any other company or organization that you pay on a regular basis. Each financial institution that offers electronic payments to merchants will have an online method to set up each of the payees.

For each payee, you will need the basic information of payee name, address, phone number, and account number. This information is readily available on the latest bill from that merchant. Have those bills readily available when you log on to your financial institution's web site. It should take approximately two to three minutes to set up each payee account. Once the payee account is set up, you will only need to enter the amount you owe each month and when you want it paid. It's a breeze!

DEFINITIONS FOR THIS STEP

Sub-accounts refers to specialized savings accounts that you set up under your main savings account. They are used for saving up for big ticket items such as real estate taxes, vacations, car repairs, home repairs, etc.

Auto Pay refers to automatic electronic payment taken from your checking account to the merchant (e.g., mortgage payment).

Auto Transfer refers to automatic electronic transfer from one account to another (e.g., savings or investments).

eCheck refers to user-initiated electronic check or transfer from your checking account to merchant (e.g., utilities).

Payee refers to a merchant or creditor to whom you owe money.

BUDGETING FORMS REFERENCED

- Budget Plan Form

BEFORE PROCEEDING

I have developed my budget on the hardcopy form or via the MS Excel spreadsheet:

Yes ______No _______

I have set up my various "sub-accounts" or single saving account to accommodate my big ticket categories (e.g. real estate taxes, vacations, car repairs, home repairs, etc.):

Yes ______No _______

I have set up my various "payees" via my financial institution's web banking system (e.g. mortgage company, utility companies, credit card companies, etc.):

Yes ______No _______

I have eliminated all third party access to my checking account. I'm in control of my checking account!

Yes ______No _______

9
STEP FIVE
PAY OFF DEBT

So far you have gathered all the information, recorded it on the forms, analyzed it, and set up your accounts. You now have everything you need to begin paying off your debts, at an accelerated pace. I've done it myself and it takes work, sacrifice, and sometimes an extra job, if you are short on cash every month, but it is achievable.

Depending on the amount of debt you are carrying and how many loans or credit cards you have, it could take anywhere from several months to two to three years to pay it off. It all depends on your income and how much extra cash you can apply each month. Do not get discouraged. At the end of this chapter, I have repeated some easy ways to save money each month (carry-over from *Chapter 2*). There are additional resources listed in the *Appendix*.

The key to paying off the debt as quick as possible is: **the more cash you can free up at the end of the month and apply to outstanding debts, the faster**

it will be eliminated. Just imagine what you will be able to do with that extra cash once all the debts are paid off!

THE DEBT ELIMINATION FORM

The last form is the Debt Elimination form. It consists of two charts, the first being a summary of your current debts listed by category. MS Excel spreadsheet users will see this information as carryover from the Debt form. Hardcopy users will need to enter the data in the first chart.

On the second chart, the presentation of the debt line items is formatted so that the smallest Payoff Amount is the first line item, the second smallest Payoff Amount is the second line item, etc. In the spreadsheet version, the sorting is done by clicking on one of the down arrows in the upper chart and selecting "ascending" order. Hardcopy users will just reenter the information using visual inspection and sequence the lower chart to show the smallest Payoff Amount first.

The next step is to add any money you have left over at the end of the month to the first line item debt (lowest payoff amount). The amount left over at the end of the month shows up in the orange cell for spreadsheet users and will be added automatically. Hardcopy users, simply renter the number from the orange cell on the Budget Plan form.

You will now have a much larger (hopefully) monthly payment on your smallest debt and can enjoy watching it disappear quickly as you make these higher payments each month. Once that debt is paid off you will be repeating the entire sequence for the next lowest Payoff Amount debt until all the non-mortgage debt is GONE.

If you didn't show an excess or "delta" on your Budget Plan form and have debt to pay off, you need to do one of two things (or both):

- Eliminate or reduce some discretionary spending
- Review Chapter 2 and the Additional Resources in the Appendix!!!
- Raise your income by working more hours, adding a second job, or asking your boss for a raise

You now know where you stand and what needs to be done. You now have a **GRASP** on your budget! The next part of this workbook will focus on the discipline you need to keep this process going each month.

BUDGETING FORMS REFERENCED

- Debt Elimination form

BEFORE PROCEEDING

I have listed my debts from smallest to largest:

Yes ______No _______

I have applied any extra cash to the smallest debt, so that it gets paid off quickly:

Yes ______No _______

I have stopped using credit cards for any new purchases:

Yes ______No _______

If I need to generate cash at the end of the month to pay off debt faster, I will cut my discretionary spending by:

____

____

____

____

____

____

____

____

____

____

PART III
DISCIPLINE

REAP THE REWARDS

"Talent without discipline is like an octopus on roller skates. There's plenty of movement, but you never know if it's going to be forward, backwards, or sideways."
- H. Jackson Brown, Jr. -

I love this quote because it reminds me of myself before I had my budget in place! There's nothing worse than having the knowledge, but not applying it. This is the third key to the whole process: If you discipline yourself to do what's in this workbook on a monthly basis, you will have completed the circle.

In these last two chapters, I will discuss **Discipline** and then summarize the ***Motivation, Knowledge, and Discipline*** themes. Together, these three inter-related concepts is as key as the 5-step **"Get a GRASP..."** process. Together, they will rock your financial world - in a good way!

Discipline yourself to "Keep It Going" and then "Share It" with someone you love.

When you apply the knowledge of the budgeting process on a consistent basis, you will see your debts decreasing and financial goals being met.

NOTES

10
MONTHLY REVIEWS

So far, I've covered two main parts: ***Motivation and Knowledge***. Both are key to overall success. But there's a third component that is just as important and brings everything together. It's the discipline to take what you now know, and apply it on a regular basis. The old saying of "repeat, repeat and then repeat again" certainly applies. By repeating this process each month, you will gain the discipline.

DISCIPLINE

Why discipline? Because without it, you are very likely to quickly fall back to the old ways of doing things. You will be back to overspending, increasing debt, and not able to reach your financial goals. It's the discipline, over an extended period of time, that will accelerate you toward your goals.

If you think back to "*The Motivators*" section, I described the concept of regular saving and investing with 'compound interest' and obtaining significant savings over time. That only works if you are consistent each and every month. It needs to be either a learned or natural habit. The fact you've invested in this workbook probably means it's not natural for you. But by applying the material in this workbook, good habits can be learned and maintained.

Each month, it will be necessary to review your budget, rework a new budget for the upcoming month, and striving for "net-zero" cash flow. Doing so will enable you to avoid the pitfalls of falling back into bad spending habits.

There are several things you can do to avoid these pitfalls and gain the necessary discipline. I will give some ideas and you can probably think of others as well that might work for you.

SCHEDULE IT

Set aside a set period of time each month. I recommend one hour, but over time that may be reduced to 30 minutes. Make it the same time and day each month. For example, every Saturday morning at 10 am over coffee at the kitchen table. Put this on your calendar for the next 12 months. You can always change the day or time later, should your scheduling preference change. The important thing is to get it on your calendar.

ENGAGE WITH A PARTNER

Having your partner involved with you can help with the discipline. Hold each other accountable for the previous month's plans. Review periodically to make sure you are on track with your goals and strategy to get there.

Make it a compromising and fun experience. Try to resolve any differences instead of "agreeing to disagree." Having healthy discussions will keep both of you motivated to stay on track.

If you do not have a spouse or significant other, there are still opportunities to engage a partner. A good friend might be a candidate. You would want someone that is conscience, understands your motivations and goals, and will hold you accountable to this process. It could be a long time friend, someone at your church, or perhaps a trusted family member.

YOUR MONTHLY REVIEW

Review the Budget Plan form from the previous month. Look for any adjustments that need to be made. Check to see if you are at "net-zero," as I described in "Step 3: Analyze." Rework a new budget for the upcoming month. If you use the hardcopy forms, start with a fresh clean set of the following forms:

- Cash Flow Analysis form
- Monthly Expenses form
- Budget Plan form

These forms need to be updated each month. If you are using the MS Excel spreadsheet version, retrieve the file from the previous month from your hard drive, do a "save as" and enter a new file name, e.g. name_budget_30 sept 09.

Refer to the previous **"Get a GRASP..."** chapters if necessary, as a review on how to complete the forms.

It's a good idea to refer back to the "Before Proceeding" section at the end of *Part 1:The Motivators*. Review the questions pertaining to your motivations and financial goals. Has anything changed? Are you on track or do need to make any adjustments to your budget? Your motivations and goals will be the driving force for keeping your monthly budget "in tune."

KEEPING A "ROLLING" RECORD OF EACH MONTH

I also recommend starting a binder and filling it with each month's forms with a tab in-between. As the months go by you'll have a great record of where you are and where you've been...nothing like seeing your progress over time.

If there is any change in your motivations or goals, record those on a new form and keep track in the same binder.

For MS Excel spreadsheet users, simply print out the complete set of forms for that month for a hardcopy record. You can then use the same binder strategy to file those forms and easily track monthly progress. Even though you have the spreadsheet stored on the computer, I think it's more convenient to flip through a binder than it is to opening multiple files on your computer desktop.

The monthly discipline of budgeting and the visual inspection of your monthly progress will help keep you motivated to stay on track.

With these three success factors and the **"Get a GRASP..."** process under your belt, you are on a roll!

11

PUT IT ALL TOGETHER

I believe there are some basic truths in life that are also applicable to the subject matter of personal budgeting:

- If there isn't a will, it won't happen.
- If you want to achieve something, but don't have the knowledge, you must acquire it.
- Good things in life usually take time

When I think of those life-truths, they certainly apply to personal financial budgeting. If you don't have the will to budget, it won't happen. If you don't have the knowledge to budget, you must acquire it. Even with the will and knowledge, it will still take consistency over time. I broke this down to three key success factors which then became the three main parts of this workbook:

- Motivation
- Knowledge
- Discipline

MOTIVATION

Half of the battle to getting started with the **"Get a GRASP..."** method or any other budgeting method is making the decision to get started. If you can't envision the benefits, you won't be motivated.

In *Chapter 1: Introduction,* I showed you several examples of how shaving just $100 or $200 from your monthly budget, and if invested consistently over time, can yield a sizable nest egg. I also talked about saving for an emergency fund to thwart off any life-crisis event such as an illness or job layoff. Finally, I talked about putting your new found cash towards saving for other fun things, such as a vacation, new furniture, or other financial goals you may have. Those are all potential motivators. For you to be motivated, it's essential to identify what's most important to you and prioritize that list on a regular basis.

Then in *Chapter 2: My Decisions,* I discussed making several key decisions that may be critical to reaching your financial goals. Please go back to the end of *Chapter 2* and review the "Before Proceeding" section. You should have made several decisions of commitment. Please review those on a regular basis.

KNOWLEDGE

A quick review of the 5-step **"Get a GRASP..."** process that I covered in *Chapters 3, 4, 5, 7, and 8:*

Gather all your financial data
Record
Analyze
Set Up Budget and Accounts
Pay Off Debt

By understanding and applying this process, you will acquire the knowledge necessary to achieve your financial goals. It will take about three months to get a good feel for this process and develop a 'net-zero' monthly budget. By repeating the process month after month, you will gain the knowledge by default.

A hint for faster learning is to use the MS Excel spreadsheet version. As I've mentioned previously, you will be able to enter data faster, run more scenarios, and quickly correct any errors. You will spend about 80% less time entering data and doing math calculations from one month to the next. It is well worth the extra investment just from a time savings standpoint.

DISCIPLINE

I covered *Discipline* in the last chapter, so it should be fresh. The keys to that chapter were:

- Schedule It
- Engage With a Partner
- Monthly Reviews
- Keep a "Rolling Record of Each Month"

Having the discipline to put your motivations and new-found knowledge into action will set you apart from your friends, family and co-workers. Don't delay a minute, put this stuff into action AND keep it going EVERY month.

PUT IT ALL TOGETHER...AND KEEP IT GOING!

Putting ***Motivation, Knowledge, and Discipline*** together will get you on a healthy track with budgeting and, ultimately, with financial goals. I strongly believe these three success factors feed off each other. If you do only two of the three, you greatly reduce the chance for success. Think of these three factors as a chain link. If any of the links is broken, the chain is broken.

Another way to look at is through the circle diagram below. You are in the middle. Now you have the ***Motivation, Knowledge, and the Discipline.***

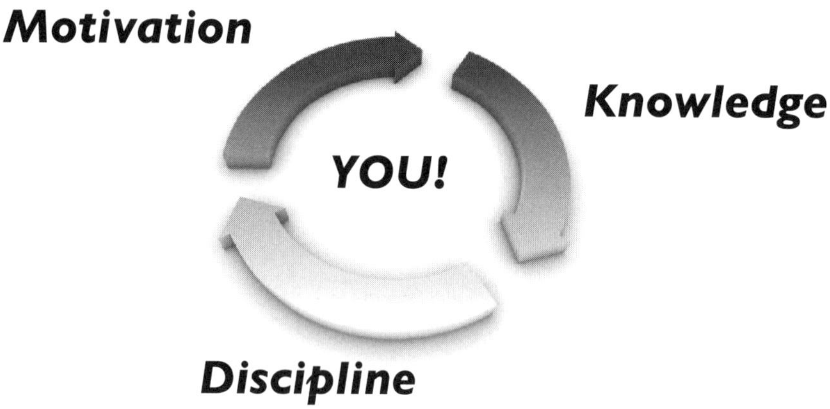

There's only one thing left to do...***Share It!***...with your loved ones and especially your children.

12
SHARE IT!

Now that you **"Got the GRASP...,"** please share it with someone you love. What could be more special than sharing a gift that will keep on giving? In this chapter, I'll cover a few other areas of your friends or family members that could greatly benefit.

Of utmost importance is your children. Now that you've changed your financial life for the better and forever, spread the love to your children. Make this a family commitment so everyone is on the same page and benefiting together.

"GET A GRASP..." FOR KIDS (THE KID'S REWARD PROGRAM)

They don't teach this stuff in school, that's for sure! You would be doing your kids and grandkids a favor by sharing this information with them, although slightly on a different scale.

I would like to share a program that I did for my son, starting when he was about 10 years old. I would have started earlier, if I had known better! I am a real proponent of starting youth with some basic expectations and structure. I think you will find it invaluable in shaping your child's behavior and appreciation for money.

There are basically two stages:

- *Early Stage* (old enough to do chores, but not working outside the home)
- *Later Stage* (living at home, but working outside the home)

KID'S PROGRAM - EARLY STAGE

In the *Early Stage*, I used a monetary reward program. No weekly spending "allowances" in my home! I set up a list of behavior expectations and chores and posted it on the kitchen refrigerator each week. The behavior expectations were things such as:

- Obeying without arguing
- Personal hygiene without arguing (e.g. brushing teeth, bath, shower, etc.)
- Homework before playtime or TV

There was no monetary award program for those behavior expectations. But the chore list did have a monetary reward attached. The award was typically between $.50 to $1.00. The chores varied based on his age and abilities, but examples included:

- Cleaning room (including dusting and vacuuming)
- Vacuuming other rooms in the house
- Cleaning the bathroom (yes, everything)
- Emptying the dishwasher
- Cleaning the garage
- Taking out the garbage
- Mowing the lawn

Having a clear list of chores and a monetary reward attached to them, taught at an early age that if he wanted some nice treats, he could earn them by doing those chores. Each time he accomplished a chore, we checked it off and added the agreed amount to his weekly bottom line. When he had enough money saved, he was allowed to buy the extra toy or treat.

In the ***Kid's Reward Program*** in the *Appendix,* you will see a sample form that you can use as is, or modify to suit your specific situation.

One further note on the Early Stage. If you have a difficult behavior situation with a child, you probably need to address the behavior issues first, before the chore and monetary reward program will be effective. If you would like further assistance in the behavior expectation area, I highly recommend a program called **The Total Transformation** by James Lehman, MSW, Behavioral Therapist. His website is http://www.thetotaltransformation.com. James provides countless tools for parents to use to address early behavioral issues.

KID'S PROGRAM - LATER STAGE

For the *Later Stage* when the child is living at home and earning an income from a part time job, there is a subset of the "Get a GRASP..." program that is very applicable. It's never too early to start a child with a budgeting program. They won't learn this in high school or college, so it's imperative that this teaching comes from a parent.

For working teens, I recommend using a cash envelope system with just a few budget categories. Teens don't have the extensive bill paying requirements such as utilities, mortgages, or multiple other payments that justify an electronic banking system.

I recommend identifying a few budget categories and creating an envelop for each one. Examples include:

- Car Expense, gas
- Car Expense, insurance
- Social Activities
- Clothing
- Charitable Giving
- Saving

For convenience, the *Income Form and the Budget Plan Form* can be used to help work through the math. It should only take about 15-20 minutes to work out a simple budget for a teen's income.

By creating an envelope for each category, carving up their paycheck into the appropriate cash amounts, your teen will essentially be living on a budget!

Besides our children, there are many other family members or friends that could benefit from this program. I'll conclude this chapter and this workbook with a few examples...

"GET A GRASP..." FOR NEWLYWEDS

What a joyous occasion! Nothing can be more exciting that starting a brand new life from scratch with a partner. It is the perfect time to get on sound financial footing. The **"Get a GRASP..."** system is a perfect opportunity for partners to sit down together, put their information together in a meaningful format, set goals, and plan on living debt-free right from the start.

Many marriages have financial problems down the road. I'd bet most of those could be avoided with sound financial planning up front and continuous communication. These tools and output reports are a perfect vehicle to have honest dialogue. You can't argue about the black and white facts that this system provides. Better to know and understand where you are, so you can figure out how to get where you want to be, especially as a new couple!

If you know someone getting married, share the knowledge. Better yet, give them the **"Get a GRASP..."** program as a gift. It will keep on giving for the rest of their lives!

"GET A GRASP..." FOR SINGLES

Singles need to plan their finances even more so than married individuals. Why? Because if a single person has a life setback such as illness or job loss, who is there to back them up? Several people I know have been through this, including me, and it's not fun. I'm very thankful to have had this system in place to protect me with minimal debt and an emergency fund to keep me going during those rough economic times.

If you are a single individual, I highly recommend an accountability partner. This is someone whom you trust and can review your plan with on a regular basis to make sure you stay on track, much like an accountability partner for *Weight Watchers®*. You are more apt to follow a plan if someone else is holding you accountable. With your finances, your accountability partner could be a parent, sibling, pastor, or long time friend.

"GET A GRASP..." FOR FIXED-INCOMERS

Just because you're on a fixed-income doesn't mean you don't have to budget! You need to keep your expenses in line because you ARE on a fixed budget. I think this one is a no- brainer, but I've all too often heard an elderly person say, "I can't be on a budget; I want to spoil my grandkids." Well, spoiling grandkids is great. But you need to live wisely also. So be careful with the spoiling and make sure you **GRASP** the concept here!

Other fixed incomes could be those receiving unemployment, disability, or some other limited reduced-income. They're probably struggling and could use some knowledge and help. Consider offering this program to them as a gift. It may be just what they need.

Building a solid financial plan for yourself and loved ones is like building a house - better on rock than on shifting sand.

- Start with a blueprint with your motivators and goals
- Learn the budgeting process and how to use the tools
- Discipline yourself and reap the reward

"He who heeds these words

and puts into practice,

is like a wise man who built

his house on a rock."

- Matthew 7:24

APPENDIX A
Recommended Resources

The resources listed below are great for extra reading or research on motivation, personal budgeting, debt management, and other topics mentioned in this workbook.

BOOKS

"Rich Dad, Poor Dad: What the Rich Teach Their Kids About Money-- That the Poor and Middle Class Do Not" by Robert T. Kiyosaki

"Total Money Makeover: A Proven Plan for Financial Fitness" by Dave Ramsey

"Start Where You Are: Life Lessons in Getting from Where You Are to Where You Want to Be" by Chris Gardner

ON-LINE ARTICLES AND RESOURCES

The Truth About Debt
https://www.daveramsey.com/thetruth_about/debt_3036.html.cfm

Pay Off the Plastic
http://money.cnn.com/2009/04/09/pf/saving/credit_cards_willis/index.htm

101 Ways to Trim Your Budget
http://www.careoncredit.com/Knowledge/101WaystoTrimYourBudget.aspx

Behold the Miracle of Compounding
http://www.kiplinger.com/columns/starting/archive/2007/stl107.htm

Historical Chart of the Dow Jones Industrial Average
http://stockcharts.com/historical.djia1900.html

The Total Transformation by James Lehman
http://www.hetotaltransformation.com

See many more articles and resources at **http://PersonalEconomicCoachingLive.com**, then select "Blog"

BUDGET COACHING SERVICES

Personal Economic Coaching Live
http://PersonalEconomicCoachingLive.com, then select "Coaching Services"

APPENDIX B
Blank Hardcopy Forms

The forms in this appendix need to be printed out each month, filled in per the description in this workbook, and then inserted into your binder or filing system.

Print out the example forms before you begin entering your own information:

- Doing so will enable you to see the finished product with sample data before you start.
- Print by Selecting 'File' then 'Print'
- In the dialogue box, select 'Entire Worksheet'

OVERVIEW INSTRUCTIONS

- Start with 'Assets' tab along the bottom and fill in your personal information in the **LIGHTLY-SHADED** highlighted cells
- The **LIGHTLY-SHADED** highlighted cells are the only cells that need modification. Simply type over the example data.
- For any sample data that is not applicable to you, simply hover over that cell, tap the space bar and ENTER.

ENTERING YOUR PERSONAL INFORMATION

- For the **LIGHTLY-SHADED** highlighted cells, key in your personal data and ENTER. You will see the blank cell or the example data be replaced with your own.

SAVING THE FILE

- I recommend saving the file to a new file name every 5 or 10 minutes.
- For the first file save, click on File, then 'Save As'
- Enter a file name that you will recognize. I recommend including a date. Ex: MyName__Budget_Date.xls
- The next time you save the file simply click on 'File' and then 'Save'
- I recommend running this spreadsheet every month and each month's file would be distinguished by the Date in the file name.

MOVING TO A NEW TAB

- Once your data is entered in on the 'Assets' tab and the file is saved, simply click on the 'Debt' tab along the bottom. Begin entering your personal data in the LIGHTLY-SHADED cells.
- Repeat Saving file and move to next tab in sequence until you've completed all the tabs requiring your input - the LIGHTLY-SHADED cells. Follow any specific instructions located on tab.

HINTS / TIPS

- The most difficult part of the spreadsheet is the Budget Plan and figuring out your weekly spend if you are not on a weekly paycheck. Follow the example for real estate taxes.
- The second most difficult concept in the Budget Plan is figuring out whether an item is Cash, eCheck, or Debit Card and how "saving sub accounts" can be used. I've given general guideline on those in the "Payment Method" column of the Bud get Plan tab. Following that guideline should make it easier to execute.
- It generally takes a few months to really nail down a good budget. Do not get frustrated if you're making adjustments the first couple of months. That is very normal.
- Discipline is KEY to success. Make this spreadsheet a part of your weekly routine. Once you've ramped up, about 15 minutes a week is all you need.
- Our Personal Finance Coaches are just a phone call away. You may log onto the website at **http://PersonalEconomicCoachingLive.com** and then go to the *Tools and Coaching Services* tab to schedule an appointment. Several service options at reasonable cost are available.
- If a dialogue box appears upon opening this sheet, click on "Enable Macros."

Assets

Date:

Category	Description	Institution	Account #	Asset
Primary Residence				
Other Residence				
Vehicle 1				
Vehicle 2				
401k				
Other Retirement Fund				
Emergency Fund				
Savings				
Checking				
Other Liquid				
Other Liquid				
Other Liquid				
Life Insurance Assets				
Total Assets				

Asset by Type

Category	Totals
Residences	
Vehicles	
Retirement	
Emergency Fund	
Liquid Assets	
Life Insurance	

Debt

Date:

Category	Description	Institution	Account #	Amount Owed	Mo Pymt	Optional Input	
						Term (mos)	Interest Rate (yr)
Primary Residence							
Other Residence							
Home Equity loans							
Timeshares							
Vehicle 1							
Vehicle 2							
Credit Card 1							
Credit Card 2							
Credit Card 3							
Credit Card 4							
Student Loans							
Total Liabilities							

Debt by Type

Category	Totals
Residences	
Timeshares	
Vehicles	
Credit Cards	
Student Loans	

Net Worth

Total New Worth =
(Total Assets minus Total Debts)

Net Monthly Income

Date:

Category	Description	Amount
Job Income	Salary	
	Commission	
	Bonuses	
	Other	
Investment Income	Interest	
	Dividends	
	Rent	
	Other	
Support Income	Alimony	
	Child Support	
	Disability	
	Other	
Business Income	Royalties	
	Other	
	Other	
Retirement Income	Social Security	
	Pension	
	Annuity	
	Other	
Total Net Income per Month		

Monthly Income Breakdown

Enter Weekly net check amount. Week 5 only occurs 4 times/year. If paid twice monthly, only enter Week 1 and Week 3. The two totals in the highlighted green cells need to match.

Week 1	Week 2	Week 3	Week 4	Week 5

Total:

Debt/Income Ratios

Total Debt to Net Income :

Mtg Debt to Net Income =

Monthly Expenses

Date:

Monthly Requirements			
Category	**Description**	**Mo. Amt**	**Yearly Amt**
Charities			
Savings	College Fund		
	Emergency Fund		
	Retirement Fund		
	Other Investments		
Housing	Home Equity Loan		
	Property Taxes		
	Homeowners Insurance		
	Grass cutting		
	Landscaping		
Utilities	Electric		
	Gas		
	Water		
	Cable		
	Phone		
	Mobile Phone		
	Trash		
Food	Store bought food and households		
	Restaurant		
Transportation	Vehicle #1		
	Vehicle #2		
	Gas and Oil		
	Repairs and Tires		
	Car Insurance		
	License Fees		

Monthly Requirements - Continued			
Category	**Description**	**Mo. Amt**	**Yearly Amt**
Clothing	Casual		
	Business		
	Dry Cleaning		
Medical / Health	Health Ins. Premiums		
	Deductibles		
	Out of Pocket		
	Disability Ins.		
	Life Ins.		
Personal	Haircuts		
	Cosmetics		
	Toilitries		
	Subscriptions		
	Membership fees		
	Education (tuition)		
	Christmas gifts		
	Birthday gifts		
	Other gifts		
	Child care		
Recreation	Entertainment		
	Vacations		
Other Debts			
Totals			
Total Expenses per Month			

Cash Flow Analysis

Date:

Spending Analysis by Category

Category	Subtotal by Category	% of Total Net Mo. Income	General Guideline %	Delta from Guideline
Charities			10.0%	
Savings			10.0%	
Housing			35.0%	
Utilities			10.0%	
Food			10.0%	
Transportation			12.0%	
Clothing			2.0%	
Medical / Health			5.0%	
Personal			2.0%	
Recreation			4.0%	
Debts			0.0%	
Left Over				
Total				

Income vs Spending Analysis

Total Net Monthly Income		
Total Expenses per Month		
Delta		

For **POSITIVE** Delta amounts, follow the strategy below:

1) Pay off any remaining debt (see Debt Elimination page)
2) Save to your Emergency Fund
3) Plan for Retirement
4) Plan for kids college

For **NEGATIVE** Delta amounts, you are spending more than you bring in. Follow the strategy below:

1) Reduce your monthly variable expenses such as clothing, personal items, recreation, restaurants, etc.
2) Generate more income by selling some unused household items
3) Get a 2nd job so you can get the expenses and debt under control

Ideally, after all debts are eliminated, you should have a delta of ZERO each month as each dollar of income is allocated to a particular spend category. It generally takes several months to refine your spending habits to track to ZERO.

Budget Plan

Date:

Monthly Requirements				Weekly Budget Plan					Payment Method *
Category	**Description**	**Amount**	**Yearly Amt**	**Week 1**	**Week 2**	**Week 3**	**Week 4**	**Week 5**	**How Payed?**
Charities									Auto Pay
									Auto Pay
									Auto Pay
Savings	College Fund								Auto Transfer
	Emergency Fund								Auto Transfer
	Retirement Fund								Auto Transfer
	Other Investments								Auto Transfer
Housing	Home Equity Loan								Auto Pay
	Property Taxes								eCheck / S-A
	Homeowners Insurance								eCheck / S-A
	Grass cutting								Cash
	Landscaping								eCheck / S-A
Utilities	Electric								eCheck
	Gas								eCheck
	Water								eCheck
	Cable								eCheck
	Phone								eCheck
	Mobile Phone								eCheck
	Trash								eCheck
Food	Store bought food and households								Cash
	Restaurant								Cash
Transportation	Vehicle #1								Auto Pay
	Vehicle #2								Auto Pay
	Gas and Oil								Cash
	Repairs and Tires								Debit Card / S-A
	Car Insurance								eCheck
	License Fees								eCheck / S-A

Continued next page…

* Definition of Payment Methods

Type	Definition	When Used	Ex:
Auto Pay	Automatic electronic payment taken from your checking account to merchant	When bill occurs monthly and are identical pymts.	Mortgage
Auto Transfer	Automatic electronic transfer from one account to another	When transfering to another account a set amount each month	Savings, Investments
eCheck	User-initiated electronic transfer from your checking account to merchant	When paying	Utilities
Debit Card	Card used pay for a retail transaction by debiting your checking account	Only when cash or eCheck method is not practical	On-line Purchases
Cash	You know…good ole' bills and coins!	Whenever possible!	Food, Gas, Clothing, etc

What is a "Sub-Account"

Type	Definition	When Used	Ex:
S-A	A secondary account to your savings account. Can either be separate account or "sub" to the main account.	Use to save money for irregular bill payments.	Real Estate taxes,Car Repairs

Budget Plan - Cont'd

Monthly Requirements				Weekly Budget Plan					Payment Method *
Category	**Description**	**Amount**	**Yearly Amt**	**Week 1**	**Week 2**	**Week 3**	**Week 4**	**Week 5**	**How Payed?**
Clothing	Casual								Cash
	Business								Cash
	Dry Cleaning								Cash
Medical / Health	Health Ins. Premiums								eCheck
	Deductibles								eCheck
	Out of Pocket								Cash
	Disability Ins.								eCheck
	Life Ins.								eCheck
Personal	Haircuts								Cash
	Cosmetics								Cash
	Toilitries								Cash
	Subscriptions								Cash
	Membership fees								eCheck
	Education (tuition)								eCheck / S-A
	Christmas gifts								Cash / S-A
	Birthday gifts								Cash / S-A
	Other gifts								Cash / S-A
	Child care								
Recreation	Entertainment								Cash
	Vacations								Debit Card / S-A
Other Debts									eCheck
									eCheck
									eCheck
									eCheck
									eCheck
									eCheck
									eCheck
Total Expenses per Month									
Total Net Monthly Income									
Delta									

Debt Elimination Analysis

Date:

Your input from the "Debt" tab:

Category	Description	Payoff Amount	Reg Pymt
Primary Residence			
Other Residence			
Home Equity loans			
Timeshares			
Vehicle 1			
Vehicle 2			
Credit Card 1			
Credit Card 2			
Credit Card 3			
Credit Card 4			
Student Loans			
Total Debt Payments per Month			

Carryover from Debt Page

This will summarize your debt payments for the month

In the orange cell, enter the re-amount that appears in the orange cell on the Cash Flow Analysis page.

Based on the Cash Flow Analysis you have: ____________ at end of month.

New Debt Payment Schedule:

Category	Description	Payoff Amount	New Pymt
NEW Debt Payments per Month			

**** New Monthly payment until bill is paid off ****

Resequence for fastest Payoff

1) Resequence the debts from lowest balance to highest
2) Add the amount in the orange cell above to the regular payment of the first bill - this will be your new payment until the first debt is paid off.
3) Repeat for succeeding debts.

Discuss strategies further with your coach to eliminate these debts.

Savings Goals

Date:

Category	Description	Amount Needed	When Needed	Priority (1-n)	Mos.	Mo. Saving Req'd	Mo Saving Required at Various Interest Rates: 2.0%	4.0%	6.0%	8.0%	10.0%	12.0%
Car												
Home Improvements												
Vacation												
Other												
Total Extra Savings per Month												

Mortgage Analyzer: 15-Yr vs 30-Yr

Date:

Loan Amount	Interest Rate	30-Yr Mo Pymt	Total Interest Paid	15-Yr Mo Pymt	Total Interest Paid	Delta
$200,000	6.00%	-1199.10	-$631,676	-1687.71	-$503,788	-$127,888
	5.75%	-1167.15	-$620,172	-1660.82	-$498,948	-$121,225
	5.50%	-1135.58	-$608,808	-1634.17	-$494,150	-$114,658
	5.25%	-1104.41	-$597,587	-1607.76	-$489,396	-$108,191
	5.00%	-1073.64	-$586,512	-1581.59	-$484,686	-$101,826
	4.75%	-1043.29	-$575,586	-1555.66	-$480,019	-$95,567
	4.50%	-1013.37	-$564,813	-1529.99	-$475,398	-$89,416
	4.25%	-983.88	-$554,197	-1504.56	-$470,820	-$83,376
	4.00%	-954.83	-$543,739	-1479.38	-$466,288	-$77,451

Loan Amount	Interest Rate	30-Yr Mo Pymt	Total Interest Paid	15-Yr Mo Pymt	Interest Paid	Delta
$100,000	6.00%	-599.55	-$315,838	-843.86	-$251,894	-$63,944
	5.75%	-583.57	-$310,086	-830.41	-$249,474	-$60,612
	5.50%	-567.79	-$304,404	-817.08	-$247,075	-$57,329
	5.25%	-552.20	-$298,793	-803.88	-$244,698	-$54,095
	5.00%	-536.82	-$293,256	-790.79	-$242,343	-$50,913
	4.75%	-521.65	-$287,793	-777.83	-$240,010	-$47,783
	4.50%	-506.69	-$282,407	-764.99	-$237,699	-$44,708
	4.25%	-491.94	-$277,098	-752.28	-$235,410	-$41,688
	4.00%	-477.42	-$271,870	-739.69	-$233,144	-$38,726

APPENDIX C

Example MS Excel Spreadsheet Forms

The forms in this appendix serve as an example of a finished set of forms using example data. These are the 'SPREADSHEET' version and you will notice a couple of generated pie charts and less 'LIGHTLY-SHADED' cells because data can be carried over to succeeding forms by the computer spreadsheet program. You can order the spreadsheet via the website **http://PersonalEconomicCoachingLive.com** (MS Excel is required on your computer).

GENERAL INSTRUCTIONS

Print out the example forms before you begin entering your own information:

- Doing so will enable you to see the finished product with sample data before you start.
- Print by Selecting 'File' then 'Print'
- In the dialogue box, select 'Entire Worksheet'

OVERVIEW INSTRUCTIONS

- Start with 'Assets' tab along the bottom and fill in your personal information in the LIGHTLY-SHADED highlighted cells
- The LIGHTLY-SHADED highlighted cells are the only cells that need modification. Simply type over the example data.
- For any sample data that is not applicable to you, simply hover over that cell, tap the space bar and ENTER.

ENTERING YOUR PERSONAL INFORMATION

- For the LIGHTLY-SHADED highlighted cells, key in your personal data and ENTER. You will see the blank cell or the example data be replaced with your own.

SAVING THE FILE

- I recommend saving the file to a new file name every 5 or 10 minutes.
- For the first file save, click on File, then 'Save As'
- Enter a file name that you will recognize. I recommend including a date. Ex: MyName__Budget_Date.xls

- The next time you save the file simply click on 'File' and then 'Save'
- I recommend running this spreadsheet every month and each month's file would be distinguished by the Date in the file name.

MOVING TO A NEW TAB

- Once your data is entered in on the 'Assets' tab and the file is saved, simply click on the 'Debt' tab along the bottom. Begin entering your personal data in the LIGHTLY-SHADED cells.
- Repeat Saving file and move to next tab in sequence until you've completed all the tabs requiring your input - the LIGHTLY-SHADED cells. Follow any specific in structions located on tab.

HINTS / TIPS

- The most difficult part of the spreadsheet is the Budget Plan and figuring out your weekly spend if you are not on a weekly paycheck. Follow the example for real estate taxes.
- The second most difficult concept in the Budget Plan is figuring out whether an item is Cash, eCheck, or Debit Card and how "saving sub accounts" can be used. I've given general guideline on those in the **"Payment Method"** column of the **Budget Plan** tab. Following that guideline should make it easier to execute.
- It generally takes a few months to really nail down a good budget. Do not get frustrated if you're making adjustments the first couple of months. That is very normal.
- Discipline is KEY to success. Make this spreadsheet a part of your weekly routine. Once you've ramped up, about 15 minutes a week is all you need.
- Our Personal Finance Coaches are just a phone call away. You may log onto the website at **http://PersonalEconomicCoachingLive.com** and then go to the **Tools and Coaching Services** tab to schedule an appointment. Several service options at reasonable cost are available.

Assets

Category	Description	Institution	Account #	Asset
Primary Residence	Primary Residence	Community Bank	1111	200,000
Other Residence				
Vehicle 1	2004 Jeep	Community Bank	xxxx	12,000
Vehicle 2	2008 Pontiac	GMAC (lease)	2222	
401k	Company XYZ (401k)	National Bank	3333	100,000
Other Retirement Fund				
Emergency Fund	Money Market	National Bank	4444	20,000
Savings	Savings	Community Bank	5555	10,000
Checking	Checking	Community Bank	6666	1,000
Other Liquid				
Other Liquid				
Other Liquid				
Life Insurance Assets				
Total Assets				**343,000**

Asset by Type

Category	Totals
Residences	200,000
Vehicles	12,000
Retirement	100,000
Emergency Fund	20,000
Liquid Assets	11,000
Life Insurance	

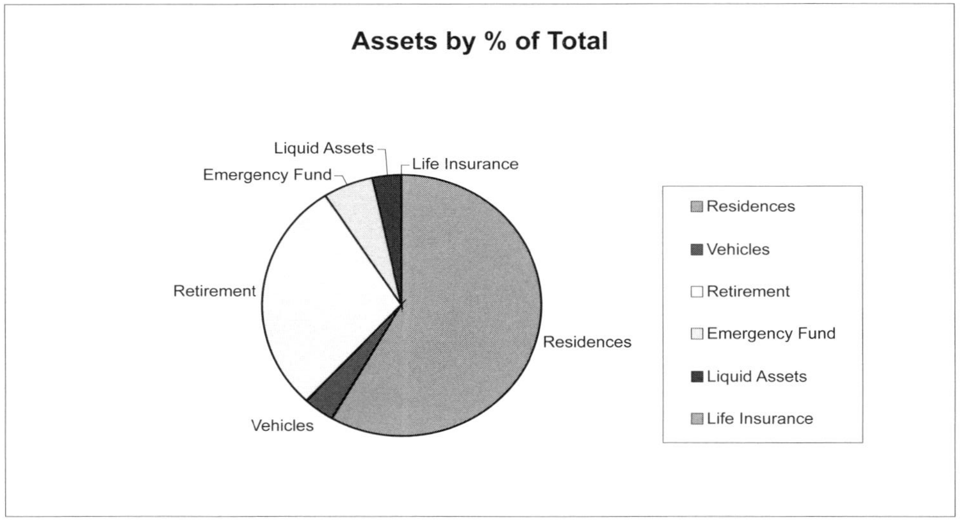

Debt

Category	Description	Institution	Account #	Amount Owed	Mo Pymt	Optional Input: Term (mos)	Optional Input: Interest Rate (yr)
Primary Residence	Primary Residence	Community Bank	1111	150,000	1,200		
Other Residence							
Home Equity loans	Home Equity Line	Community Bank	7777	12,877	100		
Timeshares	Mexico Timeshare	RCI	8888	8,000	200		
Vehicle 1	2004 Jeep	Community Bank	xxxx	1,000	125		
Vehicle 2	2008 Pontiac	GMAC (lease)	2222	7,500	195		
Credit Card 1	Furniture	Art Van	9999	3,000	100		
Credit Card 2	Tools, misc	Sears	0	1,500	75		
Credit Card 3							
Credit Card 4							
Student Loans	Student Loans	Great Lakes		5,500	160		
Total Liabilities				**189,377**	**2,155**		

Debt by Type

Category	Totals
Residences	162,877
Timeshares	8,000
Vehicles	8,500
Credit Cards	4,500
Student Loans	5,500

Net Worth

Total New Worth = **$** **153,623**

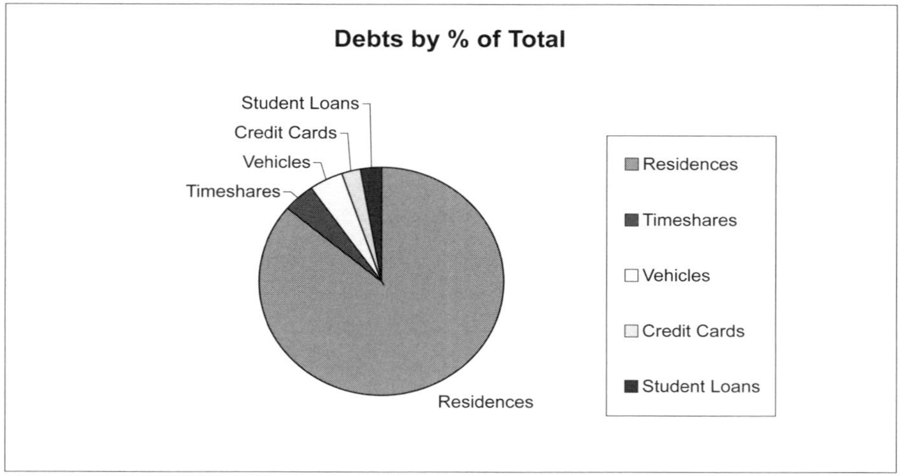

Net Monthly Income

Category	Description	Amount
Job Income	Salary	3,000
	Commission	
	Bonuses	
	Other	2,000
Investment Income	Interest	
	Dividends	
	Rent	
	Other	
Support Income	Alimony	
	Child Support	
	Disability	
	Other	
Business Income	Royalties	
	Other	
	Other	
Retirement Income	Social Security	
	Pension	
	Annuity	
	Other	
Total Net Income per Month		**$5,000**

Monthly Income Breakdown

Enter Weekly net check amount. Week 5 only occurs 4 times/year. If paid twice monthly, only enter Week 1 and Week 3. The two totals in the highlighted green cells need to match.

Week 1	Week 2	Week 3	Week 4	Week 5
$2,500		$2,500		

Total: $ 5,000

Debt/Income Ratios

Total Debt to Net Income = 43.1%

Mtg Debt to Net Income = 30.0%

Monthly Expenses

Monthly Requirements

Category	Description	Mo. Amt	Yearly Amt
Charities	ABC	10	
	XYZ	10	
	HHH	10	
Savings	College Fund		
	Emergency Fund	50	
	Retirement Fund	50	
	Other Investments		
Housing	Primary Residence	1,200	
	Home Equity Line	100	
	Property Taxes		3000
	Homeowners Insurance		500
	Grass cutting	60	
	Landscaping		200
Utilities	Electric	150	
	Gas	175	
	Water	50	
	Cable	150	
	Phone		
	Mobile Phone	90	
	Trash	20	
Food	Store bought food and households	500	
	Restaurant	100	
Transportation	2004 Jeep	125	
	2008 Pontiac	195	
	Gas and Oil	300	
	Repairs and Tires		500
	Car Insurance	200	
	License Fees		200

Monthly Requirements - Continued

Category	Description	Mo. Amt	Yearly Amt
Clothing	Casual	50	
	Business	50	
	Dry Cleaning	50	
Medical / Health	Health Ins. Premiums	125	
	Deductibles		
	Out of Pocket		
	Disability Ins.		
	Life Ins.	60	
Personal	Haircuts	20	
	Cosmetics		
	Toilitries	20	
	Subscriptions		
	Membership fees		
	Education (tuition)		
	Christmas gifts		300
	Birthday gifts		200
	Other gifts		200
	Child care		
Recreation	Entertainment	120	
	Vacations		
Other Debts			
	Mexico Timeshare	200	
	Furniture	100	
	Tools, misc	75	
	Student Loans	160	
Totals		4,575	5,100
Total Expenses per Month		**$5,000**	

Cash Flow Analysis

Spending Analysis by Category

Category	Subtotal by Category	% of Total Net Mo. Income	General Guideline %	Delta from Guideline
Charities	30	0.6%	10.0%	-9.4%
Savings	100	2.0%	10.0%	-8.0%
Housing	1,668	33.4%	35.0%	-1.6%
Utilities	635	12.7%	10.0%	2.7%
Food	600	12.0%	10.0%	2.0%
Transportation	878	17.6%	12.0%	5.6%
Clothing	150	3.0%	2.0%	1.0%
Medical / Health	185	3.7%	5.0%	-1.3%
Personal	40	0.8%	2.0%	-1.2%
Recreation	178	3.6%	4.0%	-0.4%
Debts	535	10.7%	0.0%	10.7%
Left Over		0.0%		
Total	5,000	100%	100%	

Category Spend as a % of Net Mo. Income

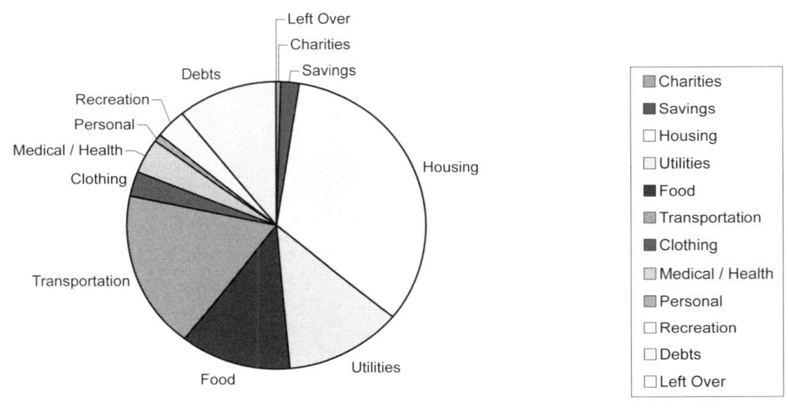

Income vs Spending Analysis

Total Net Monthly Income	$5,000
Total Expenses per Month	$5,000
Delta	$0

For POSITIVE Delta amounts, follow the strategy below:
1) Pay off any remaining debt
2) Save to your Emergency Fund
3) Plan for Retirement
4) Plan for kids college

For NEGATIVE Delta amounts, you are spending more than you bring in. Follow the strategy below:

1) Reduce your monthly variable expenses such as clothing, personal items, recreation, restaurants, etc.
2) Generate more income by selling some unused household items
3) Get a 2nd job so you can get the expenses and debt under control

Ideally, you should have a delta of ZERO each month as each dollar of income is allocated to a particular spend category. It generally takes several months to refine your spending habits to track to ZERO.

People are generally happier when spending is far below the income level, emergency fund is in place, and then goals can get achieved.

Budget Plan

Monthly Requirements				Weekly Budget Plan					Payment Method *
Category	Description	Amount	Yearly Amt	Week 1	Week 2	Week 3	Week 4	Week 5	How Payed?
Charities	ABC	10		5		5			Auto Pay
	XYZ	10		10					Auto Pay
	HHH	10				10			Auto Pay
Savings	College Fund								Auto Transfer
	Emergency Fund	50		50					Auto Transfer
	Retirement Fund	50		25		25			Auto Transfer
	Other Investments								Auto Transfer
Housing	Primary Residence	1,200		1,200					Auto Pay
	Home Equity Line	100		100					Auto Pay
	Property Taxes		3000	250					eCheck / S-A
	Homeowners Insurance		500			42			eCheck / S-A
	Grass cutting	60				60			Cash
	Landscaping		200			17			eCheck / S-A
Utilities	Electric	150				150			eCheck
	Gas	175				175			eCheck
	Water	50				50			eCheck
	Cable	150				150			eCheck
	Phone								eCheck
	Mobile Phone	90				90			eCheck
	Trash	20				20			eCheck
Food	Store bought food and households	500		250		250			Cash
	Restaurant	100		50		50			Cash
Transportation	2004 Jeep	125		125					Auto Pay
	2008 Pontiac	195				195			Auto Pay
	Gas and Oil	300		300					Cash
	Repairs and Tires		500			42			Debit Card / S-A
	Car Insurance	200				200			eCheck
	License Fees		200			17			eCheck / S-A

Continued next page...

*** Definition of Payment Methods**

Type	Definition	When Used	Ex:
Auto Pay	Automatic electronic payment taken from your checking account to merchant	When bill occurs monthly and are identical pymts.	Mortgage
Auto Transfer	Automatic electronic transfer from one account to another	When transfering to another account a set amount each month	Savings, Investments
eCheck	User-initiated electronic transfer from your checking account to merchant	When paying	Utilities
Debit Card	Card used pay for a retail transaction by debiting your checking account	Only when cash or eCheck method is not practical	On-line Purchases
Cash	You know...good ole' bills and coins!	Whenever possible!	Food, Gas, Clothing,

What is a "Sub-Account"

Type	Definition	When Used	Ex:
S-A	A secondary account to your savings account. Can either be separate account or "sub" to the main account.	Use to save money for irregular bill payments.	Real Estate taxes,Car Repairs

Budget Plan - Cont'd

Monthly Requirements				Weekly Budget Plan					Payment Method *
Category	**Description**	**Amount**	**Yearly Amt**	**Week 1**	**Week 2**	**Week 3**	**Week 4**	**Week 5**	**How Payed?**
Clothing	Casual	50				50			Cash
	Business	50				50			Cash
	Dry Cleaning	50				50			Cash
Medical / Health	Health Ins. Premiums	125				125			eCheck
	Deductibles								eCheck
	Out of Pocket								Cash
	Disability Ins.								eCheck
	Life Ins.	60				60			eCheck
Personal	Haircuts	20				20			Cash
	Cosmetics								Cash
	Toilitries	20				20			Cash
	Subscriptions								Cash
	Membership fees								eCheck
	Education (tuition)								eCheck / S-A
	Christmas gifts		300			25			Cash / S-A
	Birthday gifts		200			17			Cash / S-A
	Other gifts		200			17			Cash / S-A
	Child care								
Recreation	Entertainment	120				120			Cash
	Vacations								Debit Card / S-A
Other Debts									
	Mexico Timeshare	200	0	200					eCheck
	Furniture	100				100			eCheck
	Tools, misc	75				75			eCheck
									eCheck
									eCheck
	Student Loans	160				160			eCheck
Total Expenses per Month		**$5,000**		**$2,565**		**$2,436**			
Total Net Monthly Income		**$5,000**		**$2,500**		**$2,500**			
Delta		**$0**		**-$65**		**$64**			

Debt Elimination Analysis

Your input from the "Debt" tab:

Category	Description	Payoff Amount	Reg Pymt
Vehicle 1	2004 Jeep	1,000	125
Credit Card 2	Tools, misc	1,500	75
Credit Card 1	Furniture	3,000	100
Student Loans	Student Loans	5,500	160
Vehicle 2	2008 Pontiac	7,500	195
Timeshares	Mexico Timeshare	8,000	200
Home Equity loans	Home Equity Line	12,877	100
Primary Residence	Primary Residence	150,000	1,200
Credit Card 3			
Other Residence			
Credit Card 4			
Total non-Mortgage Debt Payments per Month			**$2,155**

Resequence for fastest Payoff

1) Click on the "Payoff Amount" heading
2) Click on the down arrow
3) Select 'Sort Ascending'

You will now see the debts listed from smallest payoff amount to largest.

ALL extra money at end of month should be applied to the bill with the smallest Payoff Amount until that bill is completely paid off.

Based on the Cash Flow Analysis you have: $0 at end of month.

New Debt Payment Schedule:

Category	Description	Payoff Amount	Reg Pymt
Vehicle 1	2004 Jeep	1,000	125
Credit Card 2	Tools, misc	1,500	75
Credit Card 1	Furniture	3,000	100
Student Loans	Student Loans	5,500	160
Vehicle 2	2008 Pontiac	7,500	195
Timeshares	Mexico Timeshare	8,000	200
Home Equity loans	Home Equity Line	12,877	100
Primary Residence	Primary Residence	150,000	1,200
Credit Card 3			
Credit Card 4			
NEW Total non-Mortgage Debt Payments per Month			**$2,155**

**** New Monthly payment until bill is paid off ****

Discuss with your coach strategies to eliminate these debts. If there is ZERO money left over at end of month you will need to cut back on some other categories, gain a temporary part time job, or sell unwanted items to raise cash. The objective is to pay these debts as quickly as possible.

Savings Goals

							Mo Saving Required at Various Interest Rates					
Category	**Description**	**Amount Needed**	**When Needed**	**Priority (1-n)**	**Mos.**	**Mo. Saving Req'd**	**2.0%**	**4.0%**	**6.0%**	**8.0%**	**10.0%**	**12.0%**
Car												
Home Improvements	Roof	8,000	6-Jun-13	1	1361	-6	-2	0	0	0	0	0
Vacation	Hawaii Vacation	4,000	15-Mar-10	3	1322	-3	-1	0	0	0	0	0
Other	Photography Class	1,200	1-Jan-10	2	1320	-1	0	0	0	0	0	0
Total Extra Savings per Month						**-$10**	**-3**	**-1**	**0**	**0**	**0**	**0**

Mortgage Analyzer: 15-Yr vs 30-Yr

Loan Amount	Interest Rate	30-Yr Mo Pymt	Total Interest Paid	15-Yr Mo Pymt	Total Interest Paid	Delta
$200,000	6.00%	-1199.10	-$631,676	-1687.71	-$503,788	-$127,888
	5.75%	-1167.15	-$620,172	-1660.82	-$498,948	-$121,225
	5.50%	-1135.58	-$608,808	-1634.17	-$494,150	-$114,658
	5.25%	-1104.41	-$597,587	-1607.76	-$489,396	-$108,191
	5.00%	-1073.64	-$586,512	-1581.59	-$484,686	-$101,826
	4.75%	-1043.29	-$575,586	-1555.66	-$480,019	-$95,567
	4.50%	-1013.37	-$564,813	-1529.99	-$475,398	-$89,416
	4.25%	-983.88	-$554,197	-1504.56	-$470,820	-$83,376
	4.00%	-954.83	-$543,739	-1479.38	-$466,288	-$77,451

Loan Amount	Interest Rate	30-Yr Mo Pymt	Total Interest Paid	15-Yr Mo Pymt	Interest Paid	Delta
$100,000	6.00%	-599.55	-$315,838	-843.86	-$251,894	-$63,944
	5.75%	-583.57	-$310,086	-830.41	-$249,474	-$60,612
	5.50%	-567.79	-$304,404	-817.08	-$247,075	-$57,329
	5.25%	-552.20	-$298,793	-803.88	-$244,698	-$54,095
	5.00%	-536.82	-$293,256	-790.79	-$242,343	-$50,913
	4.75%	-521.65	-$287,793	-777.83	-$240,010	-$47,783
	4.50%	-506.69	-$282,407	-764.99	-$237,699	-$44,708
	4.25%	-491.94	-$277,098	-752.28	-$235,410	-$41,688
	4.00%	-477.42	-$271,870	-739.69	-$233,144	-$38,726

APPENDIX D
Kids Reward Program

The forms in this appendix are for keeping track of your kid's reward program. One form has blank cells for the dollar amounts. The second form shows $1 per chore as an example.

Child's Name:

Year:
Week of:

EVERY DAY (expected without reward)	Mon	Wed	Fri	Sat
Make Bed				
Clean your plate/area after every meal				
Homework before play/recreation time				
Monday Chore				
Wednesday Chore				
Friday Chore				
Saturday Chores				

TOTAL / WEEK	
Tithe	
Savings	
NET PAY	

Child's Name:

Year:

Week of :

EVERY DAY (expected without reward)	**Mon**	**Wed**	**Fri**	**Sat**
Make Bed				
Clean your plate/area after every meal				
Homework before play/recreation time				
Monday Chore				
	$1.00			
Wednesday Chore				
		$1.00		
Friday Chore				
			$1.00	
Saturday Chores				
				$1.00
				$1.00
				$1.00
				$1.00
				$1.00

TOTAL / WEEK	**$8.00**
Tithe	$0.80
30% Savings	$2.40
NET PAY	**$4.80**

ABOUT THE AUTHOR

Michael T. Kastler, a single parent of two children, is a 1984 graduate of Lawrence Technological University with a degree in Mathematics and Computer Science. He also attended Harvard Business School for Executive Education in 1999. Michael has been interested in personal finance ever since he graduated from college and has worked with many third-party programs to develop his personal budgets over the past 25 years.

While leading a number of small groups in the study of a robust nationally acclaimed personal financial program, Michael discovered that something was missing. After investing $100 to $200 on seminars and other related programs, participants were still having difficulty developing the first step to any personal financial success - their personal budget.

Michael has taken his two life passions - personal budgeting and coaching - to a new level. Using his mathematics education, practical experience, and "personal feel" after 4+ years leading others in the area of budgeting, he created this easy-to-use process, workbook and related computer spreadsheet, for the average American just trying to survive in these uncertain economic times.

"My goal is for you to succeed in developing a monthly spending plan and have money left over at the end of the month - to save, invest, enjoy, and give back to the community."

— Michael T. Kastler

"Honor the Lord with your possessions, And with the firstfruits of all your increase; So your barns will be filled with plenty, And your vats will overflow with new wine."
Proverbs 3:9-10